THE EGGSHELL EFFECT

Copyright © 2020 Joel Holc

ISBN: 978-1-7323621-2-3
Joel Holc / Motivation Champs

The book was manufactured
in the United States of America.

To order additional copies or bulk order contact the publisher,
Motivation Champs Publishing. www.motivationchamps.com

Disclaimer:

The stories in this book reflect the author's recollection of events. Some names, locations, identifying characteristics, and specifics have been changed for the purpose of this book and to protect the privacy of those depicted. Dialogue has been re-created from memory.

PRAISE FOR THE EGGSHELL EFFECT

―――――

Joel's insight, experience, passion for self-betterment and reflection is on full display. *The Eggshell Effect* will help rid yourself of the past while freeing you up to find passion and purpose in your everyday life.

Mason Bendigo
Host, Breathin' Air Podcast

―――――

Joel Holc delivers his wisdom to the world at large instead of to just us fortunate friends. He is a good man, a studied man, and has had amazing life experiences. Joel has learned many valuable lessons that he chooses to share with us in *The Eggshell Effect*. I know you'll appreciate and learn so much from him!

Missie Berteotti, Former LPGA Professional Golfer
Financial Professional

———

Joel Holc demonstrates vulnerability around his personal struggles and offers first-hand insight on how you can overcome your own fears, tap into your truth, and live a life of confidence and power .

Nicole Jansen
Host, Leaders of Transformation Podcast

———

When you read a lot sometimes you don't expect the world to change and new doors to open each time you pick one up. Yet from the beginning of *The Eggshell Effect* there was something there. There was something about Joel's thought that draws you in. His honesty, his struggles, his victories. His life story alone is reason enough to read *The Eggshell Effect*. It is a life that reads like fiction with its hidden secrets, complicated worlds and careers created to keep them that way, and travels. Then add in the highest highs and lowest lows that can come in relationships, in business, in health, and in your own view of your circumstances. Yet it's not fiction, it is very real. Most people in America die within 50 miles of where they are born. Joel's story is literally lived throughout the world.

Tim Kubiak, President Venture 412
Host, Bowties and Business Podcast

———

As Senior Vice President, Circle of Champions member, and an entrepreneur who has been on the front cover of Success Magazine and appeared on Celebrity Apprentice, I can speak to the positive transformation I have experienced from reading *The Eggshell Effect*. Joel Holc has trained on stage to audiences of over 17,000 people and his words have impacted and inspired people to break free from fear and prepare their mindset for success. Because of his energy and inspirational words, I have watched a multitude of people line up to be photographed with him and perhaps share a few words. All his extensive knowledge and life experiences he has poured into this book *The Eggshell Effect* and I highly recommend for you to read it to help overcome fear, break free of fear's negative impact and bring inner peace into your life.

Patrick Maser, Senior VP of ACN
Circle of Champions Member

ACKNOWLEDGEMENTS

In loving memory of my mom and dad.

I want to thank everyone that has been part of my life journey and my awakening experience: Dalya Shchaf, Patricia Boswell, Ron DeAngelo, Nora Schofield, Peter Braasch, Yudith Bornovski, Hila Gofer, Imbal Holtz, Amir Yeffet and Anat Aviv-Yeffet, Dr. Conan Shaw, Dr. Shimi Sacks, Patrick Maser, and of course, Nicole and Sophia.

To my children, Daniel and Talia...I cherish you.

This journey, so far, has been full—and I am thankful for all of you being a part of it. You have taught me love, compassion, kindness, health, freedom, the true meaning of friendship—and for that I will be forever grateful. I have also experienced sadness, a broken heart, disappointment, and a tremendous amount of fear, that I am equally thankful for.

There are others who have contributed to this work, for without them, this book would not be in existence: the late Deborah Gouge, Dominick Domasky (Motivation Champs), Bethany Votaw, Anne Fleming, Nina El-Tobgy, and Lee Kann.

I am thankful and appreciative to you for the work you did to make this a reality. When I started this journey, I walked into the unknown, and you supported me through my self-discovery.

And to my dear friend Lee, I extend gratitude and love for his endless commitment to ensure that each of my thoughts and experiences that I had lived, would translate precisely to my readers, so that they could gain the utmost value from my writings. Through this process, he challenged me to continue growing and complete this book.

THE EGGSHELL EFFECT

———

JOEL HOLC
WITH LEE KANN

A WORD FROM LEE KANN

In writing this book with Joel, I look upon his journey and see how reflective it is of my own. We share the same disciplines of possibility, healing, awareness, and abundance in quality of life. I have traveled this synergistic path with him, and still do.

I did not have comparable experiences that Joel shares in this book, but I have been along for his ride for the last ten years or so. I was there when many of these later life occurrences took place—some of the time indirectly, and often very intimately. I have witnessed first hand his peaks and valleys, his triumphs and tribulations. So it is no accident or coincidence or wonderment to me that I am writing this book with him. No, it is more evidence for me to view life as a path leading to an open and extraordinary future.

The Eggshell Effect is an account of one man's personal journey—and we all have our own. Perhaps you will see some of yours in Joel's, which is his intention. In fact, the peregrination that has led me here to write this book with him, is a journey in-and-of-itself. But I will spare you the bevy of details of my journey—even though it exemplifies how we all have a path, not knowing where it will lead.

My initial contact with Joel was in 2009, through a transformational program called, "The Forum," where we both participated at various levels. You will hear more about this powerful education in the pages to come.

As for me, I am a filmmaker, writer, radio and media producer, and musician. It is the filmmaker/writer aspect of myself that connected me to the late Deborah Gouge (a fellow Forum graduate), who Joel initially tapped to write the story of his life. Unfortunately, Joel and I lost this friend to cancer, which led me to rewrite the book with Joel.

I agreed to write his autobiography with him because it is something he feels strongly the world needs to read. And I was riveted by the story of his life, and all of the challenges he has faced and overcome with sheer tenacity, determination, awareness, and love.

Through each and every chapter, I've been inspired by his account of his experiences. And through that, my relationship with him has profoundly blossomed, and I am proud to have him as a friend.

I hope you are as moved and inspired as I, and that you find great value in these pages. I thank Joel for having trust and faith in me to go along on this journey with him, which I have done literally, literarily, and figuratively. It is his intention that you find healing, power, and love from this work...and it is mine as well.

Lee Kann

PREFACE

"... The only thing we have to fear ... is fear itself."
— Franklin Delano Roosevelt, the 32nd President of the United States.

FDR spoke these authoritative words during his first inaugural speech in 1933. He went on to say, "the only thing we have to fear is...fear itself — nameless, unreasoning, unjustified terror which paralyzes needed efforts to convert retreat into advance.

This sums up my life pretty well—a life of terror and emotional paralysis. So what I'm about to share with you in my book is what I have come to believe about fear. It is what *I believe* to be true and all I ask is for you to try it on, so to speak, like a quality pair of walking shoes. If they fit and support you—keep them, use them, wear them in good health. That is all I could hope for.

I believe that all of human life operates on the basis of energy and that there are only two forms of this energy underlying all of our humanity: the energy of fear and the energy of love. These polar-opposites cannot co-exist in the same space at the same time.

Typically, we trek through life thinking that we are making decisions and choices freely. What is not present to us is that we are operating principally on the basis of fear. This occurs outside of our awareness, and at a significant cost.

When we operate on the cornerstone of fear, our gravest concern is to create a life of safety and security. Yet in doing so, we diminish our capacity to live—blindly closing ourselves off from the very essence of life—which is living and loving freely, and experiencing joy.

In our reaction to fear, we rob ourselves from the experience of freedom, and fulfilling our full potential. Fear is contagious and it begets more fear, contributing to the vicious cycle of an already fearful world. For most of my life, I understood none of this. I was too busy manipulating life, preoccupied with building a protective shell to surround me, keeping hurt and pain at bay.

Such a thing I refer to as *The Eggshell Effect.*

We construct these armored shells out of fright, yet there are choices we can make in life that would have us exist in another way, say, in serenity and inner peace. These choices were not available to me for most of my life as I had no awareness of fear energy. Now that I have this clarity, I am able to share with you how fear energy has impacted my entire life.

In the spring of 2013, when I was a 45-year-old husband, father, son, brother, and entrepreneur, my life came crashing down. In a two week span, I lost my beloved mother and my second wife left me, leaving me with two teenagers to raise. In addition, I was running a full-time business while battling a crippling disease, of which doctors warned me to prepare for a lifetime in a wheelchair. And if that were not enough, I was saddled with dyslexia, leaving me unable to read or write—a lifelong shameful secret.

At this juncture, I could barely function. I felt abandoned and completely hopeless. I had always been afraid in life, but by now I was utterly petrified. I wanted to die. And yet, somehow, inside this desperation, I found the courage to ask myself this profound question:

How did I get here?

Asking myself this question was horrific. It would have been easier to blame others for doing me wrong and being the source of my spiral into the abyss. I was so fearful of being responsible and accountable for myself. Still, I asked the tough question—how did Joel get here? It was in this paralyzing state of fear that I actually experienced my epiphany.

What I would eventually discover became my truth: I was not in charge—fear was. Fear had shaped every decision that I ever made and it continued to be the foundation of all my beliefs and actions, causing me a great deal of pain and suffering.

Buddhists say that the road to healing lies through our wounds, our pain, and our suffering. I believe this to be true. What I once saw as a series of crushing blows, I now see as opportunities for growth. How I dealt with these blows, what I learned from them, and how I grew as a result, is my story.

This book is not just for the wounded or the pained. It is a shared account for anyone in search of inner peace and freedom in their lives. My story is my heartfelt gift to anyone who seeks to find the source of healing, empowerment, serenity, and abundance within themselves.

In each chapter, I will share some of my life's travails and the breakthroughs I have had because of them. I am not the first or only person to have experienced such crises, but because I have had so many, you may be able to find something relatable, and through that, find value. Please use this story of my journey as a mirror for self-reflection.

In this book, I will share with you three major points. You might call them ideas, distinctions, concepts, or thoughts. However you refer to them, they need to go beyond the cerebral or intellectual. They must be found in your being. And this will be a continuing theme throughout my book...this conversation of being. This is the being part of a human being.

My three major points are; all of our actions and reactions in life come from a source of either fear or love; out of survival, we build protective shells around us; and we live life as a destination instead of as a journey. These three will undoubtedly show up as conceptual right now, and that is okay. With enough reflection and awareness, they will start to enter into your consciousness and your being. We will address living life as a journey further along in the book. But for now, I want to explain what I mean about having life—your life, my life—being sourced by fear or love, and how this lends to "The Eggshell Effect."

What are fear and love energies? Fear energy is the energy sourced from events that happen in life; from our life experiences, our thoughts, and our beliefs (mostly coming from our environment in our upbringing). It can even be brought forth from a past-life experience, although in my work, I am only addressing this lifetime. Fear energy shapes our points of view and becomes instilled in our bodies, not just in our minds. It becomes who we are and how we react to life's circumstances.

Love energy, on the other hand, comes from a place of loving ourselves first and foremost. For without loving ourselves, there will be no love to give to others. And giving love to others completes the cycle of love energy. I am not talking about intimate, romantic, or sexual love, although they are very important in relationships. I'm speaking to a way of being that is loving to ourselves and everything around us. When we are being this way, coming from this space, there is no room for fear. And conversely, when coming from fear, there will be no space for love to be present. From a love energy aspect of life, we can create a life just as we wish it to be, filled with endless choices and possibilities. And when we live life as a journey, there is the space for love energy to be present.

You may find this book to be repetitive at times. This is intentional because moving these distinctions from an intellectual concept to an experiential phenomenon requires repetition. It is the way of practice and mastery, as if you were mastering a martial art, a dance routine, an eating lifestyle, and so forth.

There is no wrong or right way about this book. There are no judgments here about your life being one way or the other. This is not about morality. I am only sharing my life experiences as a way for you to discover open doors into your own life's journey.

At the end of each chapter, you will find an invitation to reflect. And it is just that: an invitation for you to reflect on your life's choices, decisions, and who you know yourself to be. I will ask you from time to time to go back in your memory to find those impactful moments when you became shaped by fear or love. By doing this, you will be able to connect to the energy that has been sourcing you.

My invitation to you is to pause and reflect during the first reading and get connected to your experiences and emotions. Absorb each chapter and take the time to reflect on your life. Come back to this book from time to time throughout your life, reading some chapters or even a few pages at a time, because awareness can drift away without notice.

At the end of each chapter, you will find a space for taking notes and writing exercises. Often I will ask you to write down your memories of past events which will bring them to the surface. No need to make judgments about them (although you will automatically) or find any solutions for them. Just writing them down will be enough. As you continue on this journey, these thoughts will fall into place.

May your journey be one of new-found freedom, which you can find on the road from fear to love.

Joel Holc

CONTENTS

INTRODUCTION

I waited for her at our favorite bistro, Point Brugge, a stylish Belgian cafe in the Highland Park section of Pittsburgh. It was 2013, and while separated, we had come together after just two years of marriage to discuss divorce. I brought some of her personal belongings at her request and she asked me why I was being so pleasant with her.

"Because I love you," was my confession. We kissed lightly before departing, never mentioning divorce during the entire dinner.

The next day I paced the floor of my office, watching the clock like it was New Year's Eve. My wife Sophia and I were to have another conversation at 2 pm, which in my mind, given our dinner the night before, was a positive sign.

"It was great seeing you last night but I was not completely honest with you," she said right off the bat. "I've been dating someone else for a few months."

Suddenly, life stopped, and my heart plunged, sliding down out of my chest and landing hard on the floor. As I collapsed, I watched it slither away across the cold ceramic, my mind searching frantically for a life-line. And then, inexplicably, I was ten years old again, living in Israel.

My family had just moved from the city of Rehovot to the Palmachim kibbutz on the Mediterranean Sea in 1977, with its gentle breezes, great sunsets, and the ever-present smell of salt. Living in a kibbutz, work was highly valued and all the children were expected to pull their weight. We grew vegetables and raised chickens, goats, and sheep. Each of us had specific assignments carried out under the supervision of an adult, like Yoav, a man from Yemen.

Yoav was a hard-working man, short in stature but tall in knowledge of animals and the workings of kibbutz life. He was kind, direct, and disciplined, intent on teaching us the ways of the farm. I considered him my mentor.

There was a makeshift shed on the property where the animals were housed. One of my tasks was to clean the shed, which I did with glee. I loved animals and went to work daily with joy, excited at the prospect of such close proximity to them.

One day, something caught my eye. There were some eggs basking in the warm glow of an incubator's heat lamp. I was fascinated by one egg in particular. Looking closer, I saw that this egg was rocking back and forth, almost imperceptibly. Suddenly, the shell cracked and a tiny beak poked through. Then Yoav appeared, observing me observing the egg from which I could not divert my attention.

When the egg's motion halted, my eyes popped out. Seconds that seemed like hours ticked away with no movement from the orb. I pictured the chick hunkering in the dark, feeling exhausted, terrified, and defeated. What if he just gave up? He would die! My heart began to pound. Terrified for the little chick, I reached out my hand, intent on assisting, but Yoav snatched my arm, stopping me.

"Leave it be," he commanded. I was shocked.

Yoav squatted down to my height, eyeing me at my level, putting his hands on my shoulders, turning me around to face him.

"You can't help him," he explained. "The chick needs to find his own way out of the shell so he can become strong enough to survive." Yoav must have sensed my fear. "It might seem cruel from our point of view," he continued, "but from the perspective of nature, it's not. Do you understand?"

He was looking at me intently. His eyes were kind, but stern. I was having a hard time absorbing the lesson. As a child, I had a soft heart. I wanted to help anyone or anything in need, especially old people and animals. I felt connected to them because I sensed that they did not judge me. As much as I trusted Yoav, I did not want to hear what he was saying. I was so afraid that the chick could not muster the strength to make it. I found it hard to breathe. Still, I understood.

"Good," he said. He stood and gently steered me out of the shed. As we went out the doorway, I cast a solicitous glance back over my shoulder. The egg was rocking. The chick was on the move.

Thirty-five years had passed since I thought of that impactful moment. As I lay there on the floor of my office, I experienced that breathlessness again, my entire being trembled with fear. I felt stuck and trapped, like that chick in the eggshell. There was a desperation for someone to come and help me and ease my pain. It was in this moment that I found an opening to a new relationship with my struggles, that would put me on my life-long healing journey.

CHAPTER 1

NO MAN'S LAND

Technically, my journey began when I was born, and continued in Argentina, Israel, the Netherlands, Brazil, New York, and finally (so far) in Pittsburgh. But in sharing my life journey, I must begin in the spring of 2013, in what may seem like an ungodly place, Toronto's Pearson International Airport, the largest in Canada.

Like most major airports, it is both cavernous and oddly claustrophobic. With a six-hour layover to Israel, my stay seemed like eternity, given the gravity of my circumstances. The impending death of my mother and impending death of my marriage had left me in a peculiar combination of bewilderment and consciousness, frequently vacillating between the two.

I was one of thousands of other nomads wandering through Pearson International. I was not in Pittsburgh where I lived, nor in Israel where I was raised and to where I was returning. I felt like Viktor Navorski, the Tom Hanks character in the movie, "The Terminal," a man stuck in an airport, a man with no country, a man between worlds. Simply put—in no man's land.

I sat there scanning my situation. My second wife, Sophia, and I were struggling in our marriage, even though we had done couples counseling in the past. Then at her urging, I began seeing a therapist on my own to explore how I might be contributing to the marital discord. The work I did with my therapist was beginning to reveal some of the invisible infrastructure of my psyche.

Patricia, a therapist in her fifties, was tall and attractive with long flowing black hair. She was confident and in tune with me, just as I was beginning to understand some of the experiences, beliefs, and assumptions that had shaped how I viewed the world, and the subsequent decisions I had made.

In fact, I had unearthed something quite consequential. I saw for the first time that I did not feel safe with women unless I perceived them to be broken, wounded, or vulnerable in some way that was as great or greater than myself. There was a great freedom in discovering how I established romantic relationships.

Later that day, my oldest sister, Yudith, called me from my mother's apartment in Rehovot, Israel, to relay to me that our mother was dying and "it's going to end soon." I hung up the phone feeling lost, helpless, and uncertain. Of course, I wanted to see my mother one last time before she died, but it was not so easy to just get up and go. Last-minute plane fare to Israel was expensive and my life in Pittsburgh was complicated. I ran my own business, had to deal with two teens, and struggled in my marriage.

Something about this last phone call was different, however. When Yudith—her voice breaking—told me that our mother could die at any moment, I believed her. My mother, Malka, a small but strong woman with big hair and an even bigger heart, had stopped eating days before. She had been battling cancer—with it starting in her intestines, then metastasizing to her breast and liver—for seven torturous years. Eventually, her doctors gave up on her. There was nothing they could do, they claimed, except to try to ease her pain.

My mother grew tired of the fight and surrendered to death. She had faced the horrors of death before in her life, but for me, her impending death was terrifying. I could not imagine life without her, even though I had not lived with her since I was ten years old. She was the most important person in my life, and I wanted—no, needed—to see her one last time. I was terrified of losing her.

As for Sophia, she was a beautiful woman with a beautiful expansive smile and a passion for life and healthy living. While her gregarious personality afforded her the ease in which to connect with anyone, she could not connect with me at that moment. She wanted me to wait until my mother actually passed and then go to Israel for the funeral. She was also skeptical that my mother was actually dying.

"It can't be," Sophia protested, "you just saw her a few weeks ago and she seemed strong. She couldn't deteriorate this fast."

For the few years that Sophia and I had been together, I had gone to Israel habitually to see my mom—something I was able to do—thanks to Sophia being at home with the kids. In fact, she and I had flown to Israel with my two children just three weeks prior so that we could all say goodbye.

"How many times do you need to say goodbye?" she probed, then added, "you always go and leave me here with the kids."

She was right. The kids were mine from my previous marriage to Nicole. They were not Sophia's responsibility even though she was their step-mother, who worked very hard to be just that. I could understand on one level why she was resistant. It was reasonable for Sophia to ask that I not jump on a plane to go across the globe once again to visit my ailing mother. But when my sister called to tell me that Malka was actually dying, something shifted. I had to go. I just had to go. I felt a great disappointment with Sophia's insensitivity. How could she not see my anguish?

Sophia stated emphatically that it was not okay with her that I leave. All I could hear was—she didn't care how I felt or what was important to me. She pressed the issue and would not leave it alone. She stated over and over that if I left, she would be gone. The conversation naturally got heated. She stormed off to the bedroom yelling from the top of the stairs.

"If you leave, I will not be here when you get back," was her threat. A couple of hours had passed when she returned to say, "I don't want you to go but if you do, we are going back to counseling."

I felt that it might be a good time to share with her the realization from my session with Patricia earlier in the day. My cognizance was so illuminating that in the midst of this breakdown of ours, I hoped that my confession would unify us. Instead, she was incensed.

"So, you're saying you picked me because you thought I was broken?"

she queried in consternation.

I watched feebly as tears of fury streamed down her face. Then, as the information began to sink in, all of her softness hardened and her anger flared.

"And because you thought I was broken, you thought you'd be able to control me?" she spouted. "And turn me into a substitute mother for your kids?"

I recoiled and went on the defense. "No, no," I protested. "It's not about control. You give me too much credit."

But the damage was done. To my own terror, the fragile tapestry that was our marriage was unraveling in the moment. Fear had been running my show forever. I was clinging onto my mother and my marriage, but the two seemed to have somehow come to oppose each other like a competition. If I reached for one, the other slipped away. I tried to still the rising panic. Since my mother's death was imminent, I would go to Israel and fix this with Sophia later.

After all, I saw myself as a problem-solver. That is who I was, and still am. I had learned to solve challenges and by-pass obstacles to survive my fear-stricken life. That is how I became the fixer. I dwelled in a life of great fear, so I developed coping skills to get around all of my dilemmas and the fear they brought. And my greatest fear in life was that the world would discover that I could not read or write and that I was stupid.

In my session with Patricia, I had not broached this subject, but I had discovered this comfort zone of being with broken women. I had admitted as much to Sophia with disastrous results, wanting to be straight with her, thinking she would admire me for my honesty. But all I was trying to do was fix it. Rather than tell her such a thing in the context of love, I shared it with her out of fear of losing her, which is what I propagated by telling her in the context of fear. Fear had been running my show forever.

Invitation to Reflect

———

When I reflect back on my illuminating discovery of how I established relationships with women—as I perceived them to be broken or wounded in some way—I see that all of us, in one way or another, can occur as broken or wounded. And all of us can occur as perfect and complete, just the way we are. But coming from fear, all I could see was broken-ness. I was unable to source myself from love and compassion.

Look at your relationships past and present, and see if you can find the fear that is in your background. Where and how does fear source your actions and feelings? Now think about those same relationships while coming from a place of love rather than fear. How do those relationships appear now?

Pick your most prominent relationship and see where fear is lurking. Then look to see what protective devices you use. Mine was to be the fixer. This was a large part of the construction of my eggshell. It kept me valuable and safe. Discover how you have constructed your eggshell.

———

Invitation to Reflect
NOTES

_____

_____

_____

_____

_____

_____

_____

_____

_____

_____

_____

_____

_____

_____

_____

_____

Invitation to Reflect
NOTES

_____

_____

_____

_____

_____

_____

_____

_____

_____

_____

_____

_____

_____

_____

_____

Invitation to Reflect
NOTES

_____

_____

_____

_____

_____

_____

_____

_____

_____

_____

_____

_____

_____

_____

_____

_____

CHAPTER 2

DIAGNOSIS

As I wandered through the airport, I was numb, in a fog, somewhat dazed, in a state of befuddlement. I was disconnected from self. Through the haze, I spotted an empty table at an otherwise crowded restaurant and ordered a salad with a glass of wine. The restaurant was an ocean of noise pollution: clattering dishes, idle chatter, the drone of scattered TV screens, and the perpetual flight announcements in English and foreign languages that seemed to roll on forever. It was like being in the eye of a hurricane. The storm surrounded me, but for the moment, I was untouched. My fog enveloped me like a shroud, keeping me in a queer calm.

My conversation with Sophia from the night before weighed heavily on my mind. But I told myself that I would think about it later so I could focus on seeing my mother through this passage. Sophia will still be there when I get back, and then I will pull out all the stops and fix this. So that was my game plan.

For as long as I can remember, I had thought of life as an elaborate game, like chess. The goal was to win and the trick was to outthink your opponent, to anticipate their every move, and to strategize a response. I was constantly thinking at least three moves ahead. But this time, something was amiss. The conversation with Sophia had made me pensive.

I methodically made my way through the long and yawning corridors to the departure gate. I had a lot to process and much time in which to do it, which was exactly what I did not want.

The flight to Tel Aviv was twelve hours, so there was plenty of time to reflect on my life. As I raced to my mother's bedside before I lost her, Sophia and all our issues were with me. I was annoyed that she had so little compassion for my situation and was not standing with me in my need to be with Malka, yet I was acutely aware of all of her past support. She literally had taken charge of my health, and in turn, saved my life.

My diagnosis came well before Sophia had entered my life. I was in my late thirties when I first began having back issues in 2005. It started with pain in my lower back, and at times, my back would go into spasms. Initially, the discomfort was mild and I paid little attention to it. However, on some occasions, I would get a paralyzing pain in my lower back, leaving me unable to walk. The pain would vanish, only to return and leave once again.

I had a slew of ways to rationalize the pain so that I would not have to deal with it. At the time, I was doing physical work cleaning carpets, so I chalked it up to hard work and aging in general. A couple of years of ignoring the pain had passed and it began affecting my right leg, creating a limp. I carried on though, working and pushing through the pain, never taking a sick day. Through it all, I took on the attitude that my back hurts and I limp and this is life. This went on for the next three years.

In 2008, while attending Daniel's baseball game, my limp caught the attention of the father of one of his teammates.

"Why are you limping?" Shimi asked.

"I don't know," I answered truthfully.

"You're way too young to be walking with a limp," Shimi replied. "We need to find out what's wrong."

I did not protest.

Shimi, a diminutive man living in scrubs, had a phone perpetually stuck to his head. He was a successful research physician who loved helping people, and was well connected in the medical community. Immediately, he set up an appointment for me with some colleagues. Under their supervision, I underwent MRI testing and all was clear. Months went by and further testing on my nerves and bones detected nothing. Yet, I was still limping with great pain, and occasionally missing work.

I felt a mixture of relief and frustration with those negative results. Living in limbo was excruciating. I wanted to know what was wrong, but at the same time I did not want to know. While it didn't make much sense, I figured that the longer it took to come up with an answer, the better the odds would be that it was something minor.

Meanwhile, the doctors hadn't given up on me. Perhaps they were challenged by the mystery of it all. They performed an entire body scan. My wait for the results was filled with anxiety. I remember exactly where I was when they called with the outcome.

I was on a job site in Greensburg, about thirty miles east of Pittsburgh, cleaning air ducts in a funeral home. Sitting in my truck, I saw my doctor's name, Dr. Lee, on my cell phone and hesitated for a split-second before answering the call. Perhaps a part of me sensed that my life was going to change. His voice on the other end of the line was professional, clinical, and matter-of-fact.

"When the team looked at the MRI," he started, his tone impassive, "they found some lesions on your spine. This indicates multiple sclerosis. This is not something we treat so we will pass your file along to a specialist."

I think I mumbled a "thank you" and then he was gone, and my connection to the rest of the world seemed to go with him. I stared blankly through the truck window at a landscape I no longer recognized. I was devastated and I was alone.

What did this mean? I had heard the term multiple sclerosis before, knowing someone who had it. My mind scrambled. This is serious. There's no cure for MS. It is going to get worse and worse.

The thought of being handicapped terrified me. I thought of my kids, and as scared as I was for myself, I was even more so for them. What if I lost the ability to support them, what would happen? I felt trapped.

Fear had already begun oozing into my nervous system, shooting through me, leaping from organ to organ until it reached my heart. I grabbed the steering wheel as if that would help me gain control. I struggled to breathe and remain calm.

I did not comprehend this at the time, but I had been living in a state of fear my entire life with it stalking me, threatening to eat me alive. For the most part, I managed to keep the fear at bay but now it consumed me. My mind clambered for anything familiar to hold onto.

In a state of shock, I called Shimi. I'm not sure exactly what I said, but I'm sure he detected the rising panic in my voice. His response was calm, for which I will be eternally grateful.

"Don't worry," he said, "we'll figure out a way through this."

Shimi's use of the word "we" was a soothing balm for my nervous system and he came through, setting me up with the leading MS specialist in Pittsburgh. I had been in pain for roughly three years, feeling well at times but unable to get out of bed at others. Everything was screaming: my lower back, my feet, knees, heels, and my head.

In our first meeting, a specialist named Dr. Thomas Stevenson became a link to life, a flotation device for those thrown overboard, which I had been. He asked me a lot of questions, most of which I don't remember, except curiously, this one—had I ever been exposed to heavy metals? I thought for a moment. He then inquired as to if I had any numbness in my body. I told him that I did, along the sides of both legs. As I shared this information, it flashed through my mind that I had experienced numbness in my legs since being a teenager. I wondered but said nothing. He completed taking my medical history and then we had a conversation.

Dr. Stevenson, a man in his forties with perfectly coiffed hair and a business-like approach, deemed that I had "multiple sclerosis," even though I did not fit the symptomatology of the disease precisely. In most MS cases, he explained, lesions appear first in the brain and then spread to the spine. In rare cases, the lesions spread in the reverse, from spine to brain. However, in all cases, the brain is involved. In my situation, I had no brain lesions—at least not yet—but everything else fit. So, although he could not be definitive, MS would be the working diagnosis. He laid out a treatment plan using a standard MS protocol involving an endless combination of medications. I did what good patients do. I complied.

From time to time, I was required to go to the hospital to receive medication through IV. In a dedicated room, where others like me were getting their meds, I suddenly found a group I could relate to. We could share our pain and suffering, and our survival. I also had a clearer and unsavory portrait of my future, due to what I saw and what they had to share with me.

The side effects of all of these meds were wretched. I gained weight and felt bloated, and my liver took a beating as the meds were processed through the organ. Monthly blood tests became the norm. All the while, I soldiered on, running my business and managing at home. On some level, I began to accept the presence of this disease in my life, while at the same time surrendering to it in defeat.

Initially, I requested little of Dr. Stevenson for answers. Perhaps I was intimidated, or more likely, I wasn't ready to hear answers. He may have sensed such, and thought I should be wholly informed, so he sat me down to discuss what I could expect as the MS progressed.

He reaffirmed that there was no cure. All he and I could do was try to slow down its progression. But no matter what we did, the lesions would spread up my spine and into my brain. As the disease progressed, I would experience ever-increasing handicaps that could eventually impact my eyesight and all muscle control. In summation, there was no hope—this was my fate. I was to face a life of pain and increasing immobility, which I had to accept, to prepare for the worst.

"Start planning your life to live with this disease," he said. "Your daily life will be difficult, so try to make it as easy on yourself as you can." He then began to tick off a list of things I should do.

"You'll need to live in a house that doesn't have steps," he continued. "Make sure you have a handicap-accessible shower, and get yourself ready for life in a wheelchair."

My chest was caving in.

"How long do I have before that happens?" I inquired, attempting to breathe.

"Probably ten years," he replied matter-of-factly.

He was being realistic, preparing me as best he could for the most likely outcome of a horrific and progressive illness. But as I listened to this experienced doctor, I felt as though he were pronouncing my death sentence. And yet, I am amazed at how I responded when he made his prediction. I simply surrendered in defeat to the grim future he had laid out before me.

Invitation to Reflect

———

I want to distinguish the notion of acceptance vs. surrender. As I am using surrender throughout this book, you simply give up and give in, as I did to Dr. Stevenson's prognosis. In acceptance, you can take on what is so, and be with it just as it is—and is not. This distinction is very valuable in dealing with life's circumstances. Look at where you have—and still do—surrender to life, and then replace it with accepting your life as it is. In accepting life, you will be empowered around those circumstances.

I am astounded at how I simply surrendered in defeat to my fate that had been laid out by a doctor, with me having no sense of responsibility for my then present and future condition. Why had I put up with three years of painful limping? Because I was not important to myself...others were more so.

In the development of my eggshell, I could keep the attention away from myself—and my overriding fears—by giving attention to others.

Look to see where in life you do not take responsibility for yourself, such as your well-being. What are your eating habits? How does your exercise fit in with your diet? Do you use substances to comfort yourself and numb out? And do you take care of others while neglecting your own health—physical and emotional?

———

Invitation to Reflect
NOTES

_____

_____

_____

_____

_____

_____

_____

_____

_____

_____

_____

_____

_____

_____

_____

_____

_____

Invitation to Reflect
NOTES

Invitation to Reflect
NOTES

CHAPTER 3

I SHALL SURVIVE

I lived out Dr. Stevenson's prediction for the next year or so. I had a life of pain, both physical and emotional, believing that all my tomorrows would be worse. I was a 42-year old single father with a crippling disease, wallowing in hopelessness. But I was resolved to support my children until they graduated from high school.

On the good days—when I could walk—I had to use a cane. In public, my kids or friends walked beside me, supporting me from falling. Stumbling was an issue because my right leg was so numb and leaden, it would just lie on the ground, dragging beneath me. But with much effort, and as long as I walked on a constant surface, I could move at a steady pace. However, if the surface changed—say, from tile to carpet or concrete to grass—my body would keep moving forward while my right leg would catch—leaving me to lose my footing.

On the other good days, my feet felt like 100-pound dumbbells. I was constantly stopping to retain energy so I could make it through the day. Just putting one foot in front of the other was work. If I got off of my feet for thirty minutes every so often, I could keep functioning.

But by evening, I would be completely drained. Just spending the energy to walk for one day had wiped me out.

Then there were the hellacious days of being completely bedridden. The unbearable pain was debilitating. The 20-foot trip to the bathroom was too much to bear so I consumed as little water as possible. I would lie there staring at the ceiling feeling trapped, thinking my life was over. I became vulnerable to extreme loneliness. I was acutely aware that I had no partner beside me to lean on through this torturous journey. What woman would consider a future with someone like me? And that prospect filled me with a profound sadness.

In addition to being in such horrendous pain, I was terrified of the bleak future for my children and myself. The pain both humbled and humiliated me, especially when I could not perform the simplest tasks. The kids had to dress me starting with my socks, as I could not touch my toes. I was so grateful to them. Although it was never spoken, I sensed that Talia and Daniel were frightened of our future. I was deteriorating before their eyes and there was no back-up plan. They were well aware that their addict mother was not capable of caring for them, nor was her family. No, we were in this by ourselves. But no matter how scared or overwhelmed we may have felt, we never showed those faces.

Meanwhile, Dr. Stevenson watched me stubbornly soldier on. He suggested that I seek financial assistance.

"You should go on disability," he told me in his office one day. "You qualify for it."

"I'll never sign up for disability," I replied harshly, bristling at the notion of such a thing.

I thanked the good doctor for his concern and limped out of his office, doing a terrible job of suppressing my annoyance and anger. Already feeling that I had lost my freedom and self-worth to doctors and medications, going on disability would be handing over what little control I had left. That would be the ultimate admission of failure. In receiving government assistance, I feared losing my reign over my finances, thereby losing my drive to sustain myself. I had too much pride (and fear) to become trapped in this way and it was counter to everything I saw in myself.

After some months, I had developed an attitude that was a peculiar blend of cocky and defeated. On one hand, I had surrendered to my so-called grim future, but on the other, I was determined not to let MS defeat me. Overcoming barriers was what I did—I was the fixer. It was my second nature to survive and master seemingly insurmountable hurdles. After all, this was not my first test at life. No, not at all.

At the age of sixteen, while working on the kibbutz, I was painting a metal beam in a horse stable and needed to raise myself to a higher level in a bucket truck. I caught my arm between the bucket and the beam, crushing my left arm. I was in and out of the hospital for a year, surviving multiple surgeries and physical therapies. The doctors warned my parents that I'd probably lose my arm to amputation. I spent months recuperating and literally willing my arm to work again. I feared not being able to work with horses if I had lost my arm. My survival demanded that I heal, and heal I did. I think my love for horses was a powerful source in my healing.

So with my survival history, I knew in my bones (literally) and in my heart, that I could overcome MS. With conviction, I informed Dr. Stevenson that I would beat this. I said it as much to myself as to him. He did not actively discourage me but neither did he support me in something he no doubt viewed as a delusion. He would always respond in the same way.

"Good luck," he would say evenly, his eyes averted, "nobody beats MS."

It was in these moments that I felt the presence of my mother. Her energy fed me, strengthened me and restored me—leaving me with the courage to think that I could overcome this disease. Whenever I was around her, which wasn't often enough, there was always a feeling of love and happiness.

Now, as I made my way over the Atlantic Ocean to be with her and her strength, perhaps I could give some strength back to her in her moment of death. I looked at my watch, aware of the many more hours of flight time that remained. I went back to scanning my life.

Despite having been courageously determined, I felt overwhelmed, powerless, and terrified. *Had I finally met an obstacle I could not overcome?* There would be days when meds worked and I actually felt good and life seemed manageable. Then would come the days when all the medication in the world could not override the pain. For the next two years, I jockeyed back and forth between hope and despair, depending on my pain level. A war raged on continuously in my head...I can figure a way out of this (no I can't); I can beat this (no I can't). My psyche careened from one extreme to the other. During the years while under the care of conventional medicine, my health continued to decline—until the day I met Sophia.

Invitation to Reflect

————

Look again to see where you simply surrender to your issues in life out of fear. I had received a diagnosis from Dr. Stevenson that left me with much fear—and rightfully so. It seems normal to fear a crippling disease. I believe we can surrender to circumstances in life, or accept them as they are. The subconscious mind is powerful and we can impact our results by creating in our mind a particular outcome. We can also create great fear from this powerful place. Choose to be handicapped (physically and emotionally) in life because that is what is predictable, or choose to be healthy in the face of a terrifying obstacle. You get to choose which if you have the awareness of which is sourcing your thoughts. So look to see where in life you have simply surrendered, and where you have chosen to rise above what others have predicted for you.

I remember how fearful I was of walking. The effort it required was a constant reminder of what my future would hold. I was also fearful of discussing my condition and situation with the kids. We all were so guarded and protected. Now I see that the fear was so gripping, we could not communicate what there was to be said. For me, the issue was control. I had none, and that was frightening. As a chess player who related to life with three moves ahead, I had no moves to make. I was out of my realm. It was fear that paralyzed me.

To have acknowledged the fact that I was scared that I did not know what the future held, would have empowered me. So I invite you to look at fear and acknowledge it. Accept that your future is unknown and being fearful is okay. Then look at getting to the source of life from a space of love and not fear.

————

Invitation to Reflect
NOTES

_____

_____

_____

_____

_____

_____

_____

_____

_____

_____

_____

_____

_____

_____

_____

Invitation to Reflect
NOTES

_____

_____

_____

_____

_____

_____

_____

_____

_____

_____

_____

_____

_____

_____

_____

Invitation to Reflect
NOTES

CHAPTER 4

LIGHT IN THE TUNNEL

I had a friend, Teresa, a warm and smiling woman who worked at a local Starbucks I frequented. Teresa became instantly aware of my condition since I had been walking with a cane. For months, Teresa often recommended to me a woman named Sophia, who she regarded as a gifted alternative healer.

At some point, Sophia appeared at Starbucks. After being introduced to this attractive woman, I seemed to run into her quite often. I liked her direct nature and confidence. Despite the fact that I did not seek out her help, Sophia repeatedly handed me her business card, claiming she could help me. I was convinced by Dr. Stevenson and conventional medicine that their way was the *only* way to survive. I was frightened to explore any alternative healing and Sophia represented that.

One day, she was about to hand me yet another card.

"Enough," I said with some gusto, "my house is filled with your cards. I will call you."

I had to be certain that any health professional was qualified to handle my fragile body. It took some time but eventually I did call and made that first appointment, explaining to her what was going on with my body. In the beginning I was very guarded, as usual, but once we began, my relaxation emerged. I could tell soon enough that she had an awareness of what was going on in my body. She shared with me that she had done some research on MS, but I sensed something else was present, perhaps the gift of healing.

I began regular therapeutic sessions with her and that wide and lovely smile that brought a unique energy to the room. It felt like love was all around her and this reminded me of my mom. The therapeutic effects of her techniques were easing my pain and discomfort.

I found Sophia very attractive, but I shoved those thoughts away. For one, I had no interest in a relationship, given everything I was dealing with. For another, there was a twelve-year age difference, and I was convinced that she would never be interested in somebody like me— sickly and full of self-doubt. To me, she seemed jaunty and gleeful, unlike the circumspect man that I was. She seemed very open and connected, quite aware of everything around her, which appealed to me greatly because I was very cut off and shut down.

Throughout 2009, Sophia and I became friends and I soon learned that Sophia had a searching soul. She'd say things like why I would accept things as they are when something more is possible? I wondered where this positivity came from. I learned that she was very involved with Landmark Education, an organization specializing in personal development. They had a flagship course called, "The Forum," and she suggested that I go to an introductory evening to check out whether or not "The Forum" was for me. I consented, not because I was particularly interested, but because I wanted to be in her company.

At the introduction, my first impression was decidedly less than favorable. I remember standing in the back of the room for a couple of hours (since sitting for very long was a big problem) with my arms crossed tightly against my chest. At the conclusion of the event, a man named David (who I would eventually come to know very well) came over to speak to me.

"Well, what do you think?" he asked casually.

"I think these people are crazy," I said, not mincing my words. He was unfazed.

"So, do you want to sign up?" he queried.

"I don't think so," I replied. I must not have sounded very convincing because he just smiled.

"When you're ready, you will," he claimed, and then walked away. When he did not pressure me, it totally disarmed my resistance.

That night, I went home and thought it over. A day later, I was looking up Landmark Education online, and the benefits were clearly presented. The more I watched the videos, the more I thought—*this couldn't hurt, maybe it could help.* The next available training took place at a downtown hotel. I thought I could trust Sophia's judgment, and if I took the course, we might become better friends since she was so involved in this education.

Later that day while driving down Murray Avenue, I spotted Sophia walking alone. I pulled over to say hello and she leaned into my window.

"What did you think about Landmark?" she inquired.

"Oh, I signed up this morning," I said, feigning indifference.

"That's wonderful," she gushed, flashing me her trademark smile. "Oh, I'm so excited for you! When are you going?"

She seemed genuinely happy—so much so, that I thought it a bit weird. Why did she care so much?

A week later, I joined about ninety other participants at the Hilton Hotel in downtown Pittsburgh for a weekend of personal growth and "positive shifts in the quality of your life," as Landmark put it. I was guarded, naturally, but I figured to participate fully.

In the first hours of the first day, the facilitator laid out some ground rules for the course. One of them was not to take notes. Not having to read or write in this course was a gift from God.

Melissa, a tiny woman in her late thirties or forties, with an aggressive gaze and a very firm demeanor, asked for volunteers to come forth and say why they were there. She surveyed the room for raised hands, inviting those brave souls to the microphone to share on what they wanted to achieve. They brought up every kind of issue imaginable— relationships, careers, finances, sexual abuse, imprisonment—you name it. It was very revealing and vulnerable for people to share their utmost quandaries and deepest intimacies. I found some of them inspiring and some of them gut-wrenching.

While listening, many judgments came to me; *why did they do that instead of this? My way would be way better.* On the other hand, I was very touched by the openness and willingness of the participants to reveal themselves so authentically. I could see myself in every person who spoke even though my life experiences were very different. I could relate to their pain and suffering, and their accomplishments and experiences.

I experienced a full circle of emotions. I would relate but then be judgmental, then feel compassion, but then be annoyed. Some people would rub me the wrong way, while with others, I would fall instantly in love. It was an undeniable cascade of feelings. Eventually, I came to realize that each person who had shared triggered something inside of me. I saw that when I was judging others, I was being judgmental of myself. And when I was feeling angry at someone else, I discovered my own self-anger.

As each person opened up, revealing their triumphs and traumas, the room seemed to fill with humanity. Surprisingly, something moved me to get out of myself and gather the courage to go to the front of the room. Albeit quite terrified, I mustered the energy—with the support of my cane—and went to the microphone line.

While waiting for my turn to speak, my mouth went dry and I started to feel dizzy. I considered sitting down in a special chair that I had requested, when at last Melissa called on me. We had a brief conversation about how the course would play out and then she looked straight at me with a specific intention.

"Joel," she said, reading my name tag. "What's wrong with you?"

"I have MS," I said, barely getting the words out.

"That's an autoimmune disease and you created it," she blurted. Her words pierced right through me.

"Yes, I know," I mumbled, and then crumbled into my chair.

Actually, I had no clue what she was talking about. What did she mean that I created this illness? Every fiber of my body rebelled against this idea. I was a victim here of a terrible disease. Why is she accusing me of complicity in this? My gut instinct was to fight back, but I had no tools to battle her. She was very powerful and all ninety people in the room were focused on her with rapt attention. She spoke in a way that was dead on, straight to the heart of the matter, pulling no punches. I was not used to people speaking in that fashion. I was intimidated, and of course, terrified.

The phone call I received from Dr. Lee, telling me that I had MS, had stunned me. This accusation from Melissa was the devastating sequel. *You brought this sickness upon yourself* was now my cross-examination. I felt a rush of dark energy, like being caught in a vortex.

Later in the course, Melissa had us participate in several exercises. One of them was to look at certain aspects of our past. In this exercise, I saw myself in school at seven years old. School was terrifying for me as I just couldn't learn to read. I had no idea why, but when I looked at the words, the letters were scrambled on the page. I tried so hard to sort them out that it hurt my eyes. This caused me great anxiety and I thought it meant that I was stupid.

Worse yet were the times the teacher called on me to read aloud. It was very embarrassing and I stressed myself right into a perpetual stomach ache. To survive this constant siege, I developed coping mechanisms such as hyper-alertness. I created strategies and planned ten steps ahead—like choosing a place in class where I could be invisible. I was certain the only way to survive was to hide the fact that I could not read or write. I never befriended any classmates as they were likely to discover my secret. I made friends with kids who went to a different school. The fear of my perceived stupidity forced me to become a master strategist.

On the last day of first grade, I sat with thirty classmates waiting for the teacher to pass out our report cards. We sat in neatly assembled rows of little wooden chairs with those arms that swelled forward into a desk. On this particular day, the teacher was walking up and down those orderly aisles, handing each of us a report card. At the top was the name of the school, the student, and a statement denoting that we were allowed to move to the next level. I thought that all of the cards were the same, but on mine, the words—*you are invited to attend the second grade*—were crossed out with a thick black mark.

The irony was that I could not read what the words said, but the meaning of the thick black mark was unmistakable. I was being crossed out—eliminated. In this moment, this exact second, I began to create my eggshell. This experience would shape the rest of my life profoundly.

I was not welcomed into second grade. I remember staring at the black mark and wanting somehow to disappear from view. I looked around and all of the other kids seemed bright with anticipation, excited to be moving on. I stretched my neck to find other cards with black marks, uninviting them to progress. But it was only I who hadn't made the cut. I remember all the other kids pointing at me and laughing, but I'm certain that didn't really happen. They probably didn't even notice my report card, or me. No one said a thing, not even the teacher.

Usually, I walked to school and back with my sister and some other kids from our apartment building. It was a long walk and we would always joke and play along the way. But that afternoon, I walked home alone, my heart and feet heavy. I felt more ashamed, afraid, and alone, than I had ever imagined possible.

Experiencing myself as a seven-year-old in the Landmark Forum was quite valuable. I had an inkling of the belief I had formed, which was, *I'm not like the other kids. I am stupid.* It seemed to be the only possible explanation. From then on at seven years old, I related to myself as stupid. Everything I did, every decision I ever made, every action I ever took, was made from that place of being stupid.

As my vision of my youth faded, I sat there in The Forum feeling hollow. I knew this memory had importance, but I did not have the courage to explore it nor get its impact. It would take several more years for me to re-experience that moment in The Forum, and be able to connect to the feelings I had as a seven year old—the terrifying experience of being seven.

In the days and weeks that followed The Forum, I thought about what

Melissa had said, turning it over and over in my mind. I kept hearing her words, "you created this disease." I became moved and inspired at the impact that Melissa and the other participants in the Landmark Forum were having on me. I trusted Melissa's words. "You created this disease."

I had the realization that if I had truly brought this disease on myself, if I truly had created it, then it followed that I could actually heal myself. For the first time since being diagnosed, I felt empowered.

Invitation to Reflect

This realization of being able to heal myself was a great weight lifted, a blindfold removed, the concrete melted from my feet. Suddenly, I had hope and a path from darkness. I now see that this is when cracks began to form in my eggshell—the very eggshell I created on my last day of first grade, when I concocted a lie and "became stupid." Creating that eggshell constrained me for my entire life in so many ways, especially in relationships.

At the time, I could not be responsible for my illness because I was being a victim. Once I took responsibility for this and everything in my life, I could give up being a victim.

Think about your past, especially your early years, and look for the declarations you made to yourself, ones where you told yourself you were not enough of something. Perhaps you told yourself that you were not smart enough, strong enough, tall enough, popular enough, or many things where you just did not measure up. These are common in the survival mode of childhood, which is a scary place. These early decisions alter our future in very constraining ways.

Invitation to Reflect
NOTES

Invitation to Reflect
NOTES

_____

_____

_____

_____

_____

_____

_____

_____

_____

_____

_____

_____

_____

_____

_____

_____

Invitation to Reflect
NOTES

CHAPTER 5

A NEW PERSPECTIVE OF CHOICE

As the plane flew on, with that perpetual, muted engine hum and vibration, I was feeling very anxious that my mother would die in route. I turned toward the window to see an attractive young woman two seats away starting to stir from her sleep that had begun before we even took off. We began an amiable conversation, as I have always been easy to talk to. People often open up and tell me all about themselves, then confess that they've shared things they haven't told their best friends or spouses. It's just something that happens, and I see this as a great privilege for me.

Rachel, looking forty something—with a major head of long, black, curly hair—lived in Los Angeles. She shared with me all her problems with her husband and then confessed all her problems with her boyfriend. She was totally casual about her infidelity and was even flirtatious about it, suggesting that we might get together while we were both in Israel. I wasn't interested but she clearly needed to talk and I listened without judgment.

In truth, I was grateful for the conversation. It took my mind off of my turmoil. For a few hours, I could forget that my mother and my marriage were dying. After a while, my chattering companion decided to watch a sappy movie, leaving me to my own melodrama—my life. I had many empty hours ahead, so I drifted and my thoughts turned to Sophia.

Sophia was the sort of woman who was always looking out for others, trying to discover what was best for them. She became concerned about the side effects of my meds. After some online research, she began to panic.

"You can't keep taking this," she pleaded, as she read the bad news about each pharmaceutical. "We have to figure out a way to get you off of this stuff."

I had been following Dr. Stevenson's advice since 2008, believing that conventional medicine was giving me the best chance for a worthwhile life. There may have been side effects to the meds, but most of the time I felt better on a daily basis than I had before taking these drugs. I wasn't pain-free but my pain was semi-manageable, which was a marked improvement. But Sophia knew I wanted more and believed that I possessed zero chance of healing if I only worked with Dr. Stevenson. So she recommended an alternative practitioner who was a chiropractor and clinical nutritionist.

I met with Dr. Conan Shaw, a middle-aged man with a vast knowledge of his craft, who asked a lot of questions. It's funny to me now, but when he asked me how much stress I was under, I replied that I wasn't under any. What was there to be stressed about? When I tell this story to my friends, their response is laughter. They know that there was nothing but stress in my life to which I was not aware. Thankfully Sophia interrupted.

"What are you talking about, Joel?" she blurted out. "You're involved in four businesses, you're raising two kids, and you're in pain every day. Of course, you're stressed."

It took me a second to understand what she was saying. This was simply my life. The headaches, the heartburn, the pain in my back, in my knees and feet—this was just how my life was. The chronic pain I was laboring under had become the norm.

Then, as Dr. Stevenson had, Dr. Shaw asked if I had been exposed to metals, to which I replied that I had not. He was hedging his bets that I had. He ordered a test, with the subsequent results showing that my levels of lead, aluminum and mercury were off the charts. The tests also indicated that I was gluten intolerant, which went unrecognized for eons, causing negative biochemical reactions in my body, especially in my digestive tract and immune system.

"Gluten is highly allergenic, and if you're sensitive to it, it can trigger inflammation," Shaw explained. "When the gut is inflamed, the body has trouble breaking down and absorbing the nutrients from food. The inflammation caused by the gluten sensitivity not only harms tissue, but it also triggers an autoimmune response, allowing your immune system to start attacking your body. All of that stress in your system can make it harder to process metals, which builds up toxicity. And for some, like you, it can result in a diagnosis of multiple sclerosis. The good news is, if you're willing to change your diet, we have a good chance of stopping the deterioration of your health."

Dr. Shaw's perspective opened up a world of possibility for me, as I began to understand my body in a way that left me empowered—as opposed to the conventional medical perspective of Dr. Stevenson. His was that I would have lesions on my spine, which would continue to grow and spread into my brain. No one knew why those lesions developed or how to stop them. As they continued to spread, my pain would increase and my ability to control my body would decline, leaving me handicapped. I would be preparing for a future in a wheelchair—a situation that left me a victim.

On the other hand, Dr. Shaw suggested some dietary changes to heal and detoxify my body, such as stopping the consumption of foods that were at the source of my inflammation, taking supplements, and drinking a lot of pure water to aid in the excretion of the heavy metals. Now my future looked completely different. Something else was indeed possible.

For most of my adult life, I had been living on coffee, sandwiches, pizza and red meat rarely eating fruit or vegetables. And I never drank water. Sophia ate well, so when she came into my life, I started eating more whole and organic foods. But my diet was abysmal when on my own. Not wanting to cook after working all day, I ate out frequently, with me indulging my edible whims over Sophia's protests.

If I was to heal, I would have to make a profound shift in what I consumed—so that's what I did. I stopped ingesting my usual foods and replaced them with gluten-free and whole foods. I took supplements, drank herbal tea instead of coffee, and consumed a gallon of water a day.

I visited Dr. Stevenson once more after consulting Dr. Shaw. Our visit was short and I expressed that I would not be working with him any longer, and I thanked him. His only response was, "good luck."

Although I declined Dr. Stevenson's suggestion to file for disability, I did secure a handicapped parking placard, which left me with some emotional issues. First and foremost, it was a constant reminder that I was handicapped. The thought made me sick and I felt defeated, with a very limited future. I would joke about it as a VIP parking pass which the kids loved. They were quite disappointed when I threw the sign away because we lost our parking privileges everywhere. They attempted to convince me that I was not walking well enough to give up the sign—and there was truth in that—but this was a defeating issue for me.

Once the sign was gone, I regained a sense of hope, and my body started to behave in kind. I was strong in the head (as in stubborn) and even stronger in my mind (as in determined), which eventually led to a stronger body. *A handicapped sign is for handicapped people, I thought.* As I started working with Dr. Shaw, I refused to relate to myself as handicapped any longer.

I made the decision to stop taking all of my prescription pharmaceuticals. Dr. Shaw had advised me to continue on with my meds for a year, as an abrupt cessation could be a trauma to my body. Fully aware of my impetuous decision to terminate my meds, I began weaning myself. Within a month of my new eating regime, weight began to melt from my body. Since my pain had clearly diminished, I refused to tolerate the poisonous side effects of the drugs any longer. Six months later, I was drug-free.

Additionally, Daniel noticed the effects of my gluten-free diet and went to see Dr. Shaw himself. Our family diet had been poor and Daniel was near obese at 13 years old. After eliminating gluten from his diet, he lost 40 pounds. I was moved and inspired to see the trickle-down impact of my recovery on my children. Daniel is now a fit and strong personal trainer.

As thrilled as I was with my weight loss, it was not enough. My health was not declining, but nor was it improving. My healing journey had not progressed, so I returned to Dr. Shaw seeking strides that might be made. Despite his care, he was still fairly conservative about the advancements that I could make. He did not think that reversing the damage was possible.

"If we can stop further damage, I'll be happy," he said.

"You might be happy with that," I injected, "but I'm not."

Even using a cane at that time, I still struggled to walk. Since I've always been someone who had the need to overcome any obstacle in life, it was not enough for me to merely stop the deterioration, but to *heal* the damage. I was more determined than ever to defeat this thing. I had a comeback in me.

Invitation to Reflect

————

Read the signs around your life and determine what they are saying to you. There are the actual physical signs—like my handicapped plac-ard—a clear reinforcement of my disabled condition. It was a constant reminder of who I was being—handicapped. Once it was gone, so was my crippled sense of self.

Then there are the emotional signs for you to interpret. With some awareness of these signs, you will be able to read them. "Things are not going my way" or "things are hard," are signs that can lead to giving up on things because your survival will tell you "it's not for me" or "I'm not interested." These are actual signs that there is something to learn.

Then there are the seemingly more powerful signs like, "I'm in the right place," "It's the right time," "I'm with the right people." Pay attention to these as well. And do you have any spiritual signs that you are aware of?

For me, I see nothing as accidental in life. Everything is connected, as in one action leads to another action or reaction. What may seem like a mistake can actually be a stepping stone on the path of your journey, even if you do not understand its reason for being in your life. If the signs are viewed from the place of survival, then all there is in life will be survival. But viewed from another perspective, say, what is possible, then there are choices and other opportunities available that were not before (such as my seeking the opinion of Dr. Shaw, which lifted the veil of gloom and doom from my psyche). Fear produces a place of survival. Love produces an opening where choice and freedom are available.

————

Look at your life and see the places where you are stuck and there seems to be no way out. Or maybe you see the way but are unable to act. You can choose to surrender (as in giving up) to life, or create what is next for you—and you can do this in the face of any circumstance. Look at all the areas of life where you are stuck and redefine them through the view of what is possible with love.

Invitation to Reflect
NOTES

_____

_____

_____

_____

_____

_____

_____

_____

_____

_____

_____

_____

_____

_____

_____

_____

Invitation to Reflect
NOTES

Invitation to Reflect
NOTES

_____

_____

_____

_____

_____

_____

_____

_____

_____

_____

_____

_____

_____

_____

_____

Invitation to Reflect
NOTES

CHAPTER 6

FAREWELL MALKA AND JUDAH

The thoughts of Dr. Shaw and my damaged body led me back to Sophia and how she had impacted my healing and my life. Yet the mental picture of my crumbling and fading relationship with her wore on me, and I fell asleep until our final approach to Tel Aviv.

After what seemed like a lifetime of a flight, I finally landed in Israel. I said goodbye to Rachel at the baggage claim and hailed a cab, heading straight to my mother's apartment in the town of Rehovet. Passing such familiar places on the ride, I fell back into time, of my last trip to Israel of this magnitude—five years earlier to bury my father, Judah.

I visited my dad several times when he was saddled with prostate cancer, and was with him in hospice the day he died, arriving a mere twelve hours before he slipped away. Perhaps he was hanging on for me. Our relationship could have been considered distant and superficial, and yet, I was closer to him than my sisters. We had no communication until I initiated contact and reconnected with him in 2007.

I remember visiting my parents while living in the kibbutz in the late

'80s. My dad was often shut down around his family but when another party was present, he was gregarious and quite loved for his sense of humor, his love of cooking, and hosting acumen. But to his family, he was a very difficult man, full of insecurities, sadness and fear. As a child, my experience of him was quite confusing and harrowing. *Why was he so loving to others and not to me? Why was I so unimportant to him?*

Throughout his life he had been consumed by the judgments of others, as to whether he was loved. My dad was a man consumed by fear. He lived in pure survival mode his entire life On some occasions, he was a violent man, although I was never physically injured. He would beat me hoping that I would cry. I did not give him that satisfaction.

"Just cry," my sister Yudith would plead, hoping to make him stop. The beatings ensued until finally, he just gave up.

Besides the aforementioned attributes of father Judah, there were good moments with him. I just have a hard time remembering them. Our traumatic moments in life always stand out, and are rarely forgotten. They, in turn, feed the fearful life we create.

Despite it all, I spoke with my dad every day for nearly a year once it became clear that he was going to die of his disease. We never spoke of anything meaningful or significant, nor did we close any open wounds, but the conversations were a gift we gave each other. The gift was knowing that these conversations would end soon. Amazingly, I would speak to my dad one more time after his demise. This had an enormous impact on my entire life and journey.

The last time I saw him in a conscious state, he was living in the town of Kfar Saba. I had taken the kids to see him to say goodbye. My dad's girlfriend, Minka, was there and we all had a nice meal together. Afterwards, my father made a last request.

"Look at me," he said with dying eyes, "I am dying. Please have your sisters come talk to me."

I imagine that he wanted to connect with them, just as he was with me, but I did not honor his request, which I regret to this day. I did not want to make available to him the attention he seemed to need as he was waning, so I said nothing. I was guarded and had no compassion for him because I was still in fear of him. In my fearful mind, I felt like he was dying just to get attention. He knew of his disease for years and did little to attend to it.

My dad was defeated in dying, just as he was in living—so much so that he attempted multiple suicides. I was angry at him for these attempts at ending his life, as I perceived them as abandoning me. I wanted him to be a strong father figure. Once he sliced his wrists, and later, took an overdose of sleeping pills. I made him wrong for seeking an end to his life. And maybe he had committed suicide after all. He found a way to die without doing himself harm—cancer would do it for him. Finally, he had gotten a ticket out of life.

It was the summer of 2008, and my sister called to say that he was passing. Suddenly, I felt the freedom to go back to Israel, even to reside in my inherited homeland if wanted. This was the first time I realized that my leaving Israel, in part, was to run away from him.

Just as I had gotten there before my dad died five years earlier, I was thankful to arrive and find mother Malka still alive. She was so happy to see me that she stood up to hug me despite her acute frailty. I could feel the sadness emanating from her body. She was still able to speak some, and surprisingly, asked with concern if it was okay with Sophia that I had come. That very frailty broke my heart, so I lied and said yes.

I had intently urged my mother on multiple occasions to seek alternative healing. Doctors had essentially given up on her after injecting her with false hopes, and promises of new ground-breaking medications. She had been kidnapped by the conventional "wisdom" of conventional medical practitioners.

"I'm not like you, I'm really sick. I need a doctor," was her resistive response. So I let it go, not feeling confident to insist that pursuing a new healing path would have been beneficial. I was left with pangs of regret.

In my brief experience with alternative healing at that time, I encountered what seemed like miracles. But truthfully, it was just the right way to heal the body, from the inside out. It was painful to know that she had run out of time to be proactive.

At the time, people in Israel with cancer had access to medical marijuana. My older sister, Yudith, and younger sisters Hila and Inbal, told me that our mother had decided to avail herself of cannabis during the past few weeks, and that she was absolutely hilarious when she smoked. That afternoon, sans Hila, we all shared a joint—a surreal experience to be certain. It left my mom less present to her pain and in a state of unabated giddiness.

This moment was also quite sad as I was well aware that these would be our last moments together—a finality for us. My timing had been fortunate because in a matter of days, my mother was no longer able to communicate. She had been wearing a morphine patch to control her pain, but now she required additional levels of morphine and constant care. Sometimes, surprisingly, she would arise from her bed without warning, but her legs resisted and she would buckle, so my sisters and I kept a round-the-clock vigil at her bedside.

My mother's apartment was nondescript, consisting of a living room, dining room, galley kitchen, and three bedrooms—all made to feel larger with white walls. It was adequate for her as she and my father had divorced long before. The apartment was covered with Jewish artwork. Her great-uncle Isaac had been a writer and was well-connected to Polish artists, whose work adorned her walls. This included a portrait of Malka herself.

My favorite spot in the apartment was her fifth floor balcony overlooking the neighborhood. Each morning I would prepare coffee and toast and wheel her into the sunshine. We sat together while my sisters slept, mom never touching the toast and coffee. It was peaceful and precious, and just for us. For me, these were days of absolute delight. I was so grateful that we were together at this moment in time. Everything we did, even simple things like watching the neighborhood from the balcony, or just sitting in silence, were touching and meaningful for us both.

We all knew that an inexorable process had begun, so we did the things that needed doing. We moved my mother's bed into the living room, giving her greater access to her wheelchair. Hospice nurses were available within minutes in case of an emergency and they would stop by multiple times a day to make sure that she was comfortable.

Yudith and Inbal lived nearby and took turns staying with Malka and me. Hila was not as available, as she lived farther away and had three young children to attend to. My sisters and I slept in the room with Malka but in shifts, so I stayed awake all night long, given my jet-lagged body clock. And that was our schedule for the last week of my mother's life. She died on my watch.

In that week with Malka, being together with her and my sisters, there was no sense of time, no sense of work, kids, my marriage, no sense of my world in Pittsburgh, no sense of any world—just my intention on every second with my beloved mom.

For 48 hours, the four of us spoke gently to my mother while she lay silently, unable to move. She was slipping away but holding on, clinging to life. We told her that we loved her, that we were thankful that she was ours, and that we were going to be okay. She had done an extraordinary job mothering us and she was free to move on without concerns.

The night that I felt her departing, I reached out and held her hand as she took her last breaths. Each inhalation had gotten slower, then slower still, leaving her gasping for air. I witnessed her fighting, moment by moment, until she was gone—leaving me relieved, yet angry and sad.

I was angry that the medical community had manipulated her with infusions of false hope. My sadness was for the knowledge that she died with so much love, light, and life still left in her. I was relieved that her suffering was finally over, and that there was no longer any reason to fight. I let go of my mother's hand.

At that moment, I became aware of how super-meaningful my life was. Everything was so significant. I was always trying to get to some better place. I needed to accomplish or build something, make a difference somehow, find happiness somewhere. And then you take your last breath, and suddenly, nothing matters. Life is over.

Then I posed this question to myself: *What is the point of this life? What are we here for?*

"She's gone," was all I could say as I called out to my sisters. We all hugged and kissed her, and hugged and kissed each other, with a huge emptiness in our hearts—a vacuum that would take years to fill. Life still feels different without her.

Witnessing my mother's passing was a profound moment and I felt blessed to have been present. We immediately undertook funeral arrangements and called the hospice agency and the police to file a report. A religious agency came for my mother's body as they would be responsible for her burial. It was good to have a task, taking our minds off of our immense loss.

Then, in tears and grief, I called Sophia. I was shocked at her coldness. Looking at it now, I can see that our relationship had really ended at that moment. This was officially our first conversation as a non-couple, which added to my tremendous suffering. Although I hoped we could find a way to heal, I was completely disconnected from her.

My mom's death had become real for me and I cried fiercely at her memorial service. I wept for my mother, my sisters, my wife and children, and for myself. It was as if I had fallen into a well of loss and pain, the dimensions of which seemed incalculable.

At Malka's final resting place atop a large hill, the rabbi asked us to stop and look around, and be proud of the assemblage our mother had created. I turned to gaze below and witnessed all who had come to mourn her passing. I expected to see a few friends and family, as we were a small family. What I saw was a veritable sea of mourners, filling my vision with faces that I did not recognize. Over three hundred people had amassed in the cemetery, managing to arrive at her gravesite in mere hours after learning of her death.

My mother, who had been a teacher and a tireless volunteer, had impacted so many people in her lifetime. The young and the old, children's organizations, hospitals, the disabled, even a folk-dancing group of wheelchair-bound people—all had benefited from her selfless work. And kindergarten students who were now adults were in attendance. I was so very moved. Yes, my mother had touched many lives.

Malka was a tiny lady, barely five feet tall, and she loved to dance. Even when saddled in a wheelchair at the end of her life, her head and fingers would bob side-to-side, as dancing was her passion. I'm certain that was how she survived her childhood, which could only be termed as traumatic. She did not tell her story often but when she did, I listened with fascination.

My mother was born in Poland in 1941—hardly the best time and place for a Jew to enter this world. Life in Nazi-occupied Poland had become increasingly dangerous, so my grandfather fled to Russia, vowing to send for the family as soon as possible. After finding work as a tailor, he sent for my grandmother with money and instructions on how to join him.

"Bring the children and our entire family but make sure you follow my directions exactly," he instructed, "and trust no one."

The journey from Poland to Russia was long, arduous, treacherous, and on foot. Even with the arranged guide provided by my grandfather, there had been many dangers following the route he laid out. Abruptly, the guide proposed that the group take a short-cut. My grandmother courageously refused, even in the face of being divided from her family, adamantly following my grandfather's precise path. She and her children stayed the course while other family members followed the guide, who delivered them to the Nazis.

My mother and family arrived in Russia, reconnecting with my grandfather, only to find it riddled with refugee camps and starvation. At the conclusion of the war, they returned to Poland where they found that their home had been confiscated by a Polish family. The Poles threw stones and spat at them, calling them "dirty Jews." My grandmother pleaded with them, not wanting the house, just the family photos. The Poles refused.

Grandma had been so strong throughout this entire conflict and horrendous ordeal, but this was the last indignation that she could handle. She collapsed and cried in the street. It had been the first time my mother had seen her mother, this tower of strength, fall prey to the tribulations of the war. These events left my mom scared and terrified when traveling through passport checkpoints for the duration of her life.

Eventually, my mom's family emigrated to Paris in the mid-'50s, living there for a few years until they heard about Jewish communities in Argentina accepting war refugees. My parents would meet and marry in Buenos Aires in 1964, where my sister Yudith and I were born.

In 1970, when I was three, our family emigrated to Israel. My mom often told us that when she arrived, it was the first time in her life that she had ever felt safe and at home. Somehow, my mother managed to transcend her nightmare childhood into dignity and love. I could feel her love just walking into her home, showering that love freely on all who entered, including my boyhood friends. She was very generous, donating money to anyone who asked, and her beautiful heart was there for everyone—except my dad.

When my parents were about to marry in 1964, my father wanted to renege on the engagement, knowing it was not a match, but it would have brought shame to both families. So under pressure they married, remaining together for twenty-five years until divorcing. In all those years, I never saw love between them. Malka was such a ball of love except where my dad was concerned.

I was an adult living in the States and Yudith was married with two kids when my parents divorced. As for my father, he packed his suitcases and walked away, leaving my mother everything, including the hardship of raising my two younger sisters. My mother took this animosity for my dad to her grave.

After my mother's burial, my sisters and I returned to our mother's apartment to "sit shivah." For Jews, shivah is a traditional seven-day period of mourning the dead. That afforded my sisters and me time to be together and to deal with our loss and grief. It was apparent that my sisters and I each experienced our mother's life and death differently. My mother had always been my safety net.

I left Israel in my early twenties, moving to the Netherlands, Brazil, Argentina, and then to New York after coming to America in 1992. I met Nicole, got married, got divorced, and reached out to mother Malka in my time of despair. And she was right there for me. It was a great comfort to know that there was always a place for my heart to go.

Our relationship grew from there, with me traveling to Israel and her coming to Pittsburgh. Every time we talked, whether face-to-face or by phone, I could feel this unquestionable connection. In the two years before my mother died, we spoke by phone every day, knowing that she would be gone in time. I did not want to miss one opportunity to receive her light and love. I called her every morning after I bought my coffee and headed to work. Sometimes the conversation was brief—hi and bye—sometimes I sat in the office parking lot talking for hours. On those days, I wanted to shed work and just keep talking.

"I'm so sorry, I can't talk today," she would say on some mornings, as her illness progressed, zapping her of her energy. "We'll talk tomorrow."

We spoke only once about dying. She declared that she was not fearing death, but would miss seeing her grandkids' marriages and being a great-grandma. Given how much death she had faced in her lifetime, I surmised that she avoided the conversation of her dying. With her death, I had lost that connection, that love, and that light. The thought of going on without it was almost more than I could bear.

Invitation to Reflect

―――――

The Dalai Lama said that true happiness comes from how many people we touch in our lives. What we do here leaves a great impact on everyone on the planet, so live your life sourced by love. My mom did. And all those she touched came out to be with her for a final time.

Be committed to living life from this place, a place of love, so you can live life fully. Sourcing ourselves from love leaves us with meaningful accomplishments. Life is a precious gift and we are here for a very short time in which to savor it.

Take some time and write a letter to yourself. There is a lot of power in writing things down to read over. Take on writing the letter that you would want to say before your last breath, or have read at your memorial. In writing it down, you take it from a place in your mind to a reality. In it, talk about the things you stand for, where you want to make a mark in life, what you want to leave behind as a legacy. Then go back and examine the energy source that had you say that you wanted these things. Just be aware of the type of energy...love or fear energy. As time passes, alter your letter as your life priorities shift.

―――――

Invitation to Reflect
NOTES

_____

_____

_____

_____

_____

_____

_____

_____

_____

_____

_____

_____

_____

_____

_____

Invitation to Reflect
NOTES

_____

_____

_____

_____

_____

_____

_____

_____

_____

_____

_____

_____

_____

_____

_____

_____

Invitation to Reflect
NOTES

_____

_____

_____

_____

_____

_____

_____

_____

_____

_____

_____

_____

_____

_____

_____

_____

CHAPTER 7

THE WHIRLWIND

For the two weeks I was in Israel, the few conversations I had with Sophia were distant, and not just due to geography. We were worlds away emotionally. Her inquiries as to how I was coping seemed perfunctory. Mostly, she repeated the same few sentences like a mantra every time we spoke.

"We have to work on our relationship when you get home," she would say. "When you come back, we're going to a marriage counselor. We have to fix things. We can't do this anymore."

"Yes, you're right," I would respond. "We'll work on our relationship. Of course we'll go to a marriage counselor. We'll fix things, I promise. We can get through this."

But my heart wasn't open—it was too engorged with grief. I felt so *at sea*, I couldn't process what she needed. Instead, I played my chess game, saying whatever was required to keep our marriage intact. I intended to glue all of the broken pieces back together when I returned.

When I boarded the Pittsburgh-bound plane feeling like a ghost, I was not present to the world. The plane propelled its way home and I began to think about what lay ahead for me. I had defied Sophia's do-not-leave ultimatum, so I knew there would be consequences. The return flight afforded me more time to reflect on my life, seeking to discover what could have brought me to this place. My mind drifted and I thought about The Forum.

I had completed the Landmark Forum four years prior in 2009 and was very inspired, as if a light had been turned on—perhaps for the first time. Two weeks later, I attended "The Advanced Course" being held in Cincinnati.

During that seminar, the facilitator, David, invited us to participate in an exercise geared toward creating what we wanted in life. It was a practice aimed at being free from self-imposed limitations. Afterwards, David invited us to share with the group what we had created and I was all in. I told the group of about one hundred people what I most desired—an intimate relationship. Before David had posed his question, I had no idea I wanted that.

It is customary to invite friends, supporters, and other graduates of The Forum to the closing session of a Landmark seminar, which was to be held on the following Tuesday evening in Cincinnati. By then, Sophia and I had become friends, so I invited her to attend the session with me. Some of my fellow graduates from Pittsburgh began expressing doubt that they could make the long drive just for an evening, which left me disappointed. Given that I had grown up in a kibbutz where it was important that we savor our accomplishments together, my thought was: *I can fix this.*

"Let's charter a bus," I spouted. And that's what we did.

At the evening session in Cincinnati, Sophia and I sat next to an elderly woman who had taken the course. The three of us spoke non-stop about this awe-inspiring adventure. At one point, Sophia left to speak with someone, when this woman shared some thoughts with me.

"I remember what you had said in the course about wanting a relationship. I think you already have what you've been wanting," she mused.

I must have looked confused.

"You're already with the woman you've been looking for," she added.

The truth was that I had been attracted to Sophia from the moment we met, despite her dating someone else. And I had gone through a prolonged, painful, and expensive divorce from Nicole several years prior. I was petrified of having a new relationship, but in that moment, it dawned on me that this woman was right. So despite my fears and apprehension, I fell for Sophia.

One of the qualities I admired about Sophia was her openness. On the bus ride home—perhaps sensing that something in me had shifted—she opened up fully. It became clear that she had had feelings for me for some time. Apparently, I was the last to notice.

Shortly thereafter, Sophia and I had a conversation that changed everything. She confessed that she had a very dysfunctional childhood and was working her way back from the trauma through forgiveness and love. Hearing her tell her story broke open my heart.

Landmark seminars had created a space for us to see that whatever had happened in the past did not have to define us now, or in our future. We were so connected and committed to stripping away all of our old stories and finding authenticity with each other, despite the fact that I was feeling safe knowing she was somehow broken.

A few days later she called to tell me that she had broken up with her boyfriend. Within twenty-four hours, we were a couple. For a few months, ours was a great love story. Then the magic fled when we realized that Sophia had become pregnant.

Sophia's pregnancy was shocking. I was deeply in love with Sophia but I was afraid—terrified actually—a state in which I often found myself. I had been a single dad for thirteen years and was blessed to have Daniel and Talia, but the thought of raising a new baby freaked me out. We had never talked about getting married and it had never occurred to me that Sophia and I would raise a child together. In fact, what was running me in the background, was the possibility that she might abandon me at some point and I would find myself raising a child as a single parent once again.

This should have been a monumental occasion, but instead I asked—no, I insisted—that she terminate the pregnancy. *This was just common sense,* I thought. Sophia refused. For the next several weeks, the pregnancy was all we talked about. There was only a short window of time in which she could safely and legally abort. I pressured her, and every time she would say the same thing.

"I don't care if I have to raise this child by myself," she squealed, "I don't care. I am not going to kill my baby."

So I called my sister, Hila, who knew what Sophia and I were going through. She did not share my view of what was only common sense. I tried to convince her of my position—pleading my case, recounting my concerns, and listing all of my justifications for Sophia to have the abortion. Almost everyone close to me agreed that this was the sensible thing to do.

"Look at it this way," Hila pointed out, "you love Sophia and you're just frightened. Please don't let your past decide your future happiness. She is not Nicole, she is Sophia. She is a human being and so is your baby. You cannot ask her to do this."

After that conversation with Hila, my runaway train of fear stopped and my heart opened. I saw things from Sophia's perspective and felt her pain. Instead of operating completely out of fear, I experienced love for her. And then regret set in over what I had put her through. In retrospect, it was a dreadful demand. Today, I am clear about how precious life is. I would never make such a request, let alone demand it. My fear, naturally, overrode any sense of compassion or love. I was so terror-stricken that I actually wanted to kill my baby. I went to seek Sophia's forgiveness, and through her mercy, we reconciled and decided to keep the baby.

In three months' time, I asked her to move into my house with my children. Initially she balked, wanting to create a new space for us to start a life together. However, buying a new home did not work for me financially, plus my kids' school sat conveniently across the street from our house. Eventually, Sophia moved in but never really felt at home. It was a difficult situation for all. My kids had lived in a single-parent home for most of their lives. Life for them was the three of us. Suddenly, they were being asked to share their home and their dad with the new girlfriend, who came packing a new baby brother.

Predictably, Sophia had no feeling of welcome. She felt out of place like a third wheel attached to a bicycle. Under the best of circumstances, it can be difficult to be a stepmother. Our circumstances were exacting. It was all too much and too soon, with insufficient preparation. No one was happy and I was calculating the next best strategy. Pleasing Sophia was sailing the best course, as my kids were stuck with me but Sophia was not. So I took Sophia's side continually, and as a result, my kids suffered tremendously. The relationship with Sophia had moved with galloping speed and we had other issues as well. The best description for this family would be bipolar. Life was either heaven or hell, with no middle ground.

When Sophia and I were connected, our relationship was the greatest love imaginable. We were interconnected, not having to use words to communicate. We knew what the other felt and thought. Those moments were the apex of my life. Just holding her hand, I felt partnered, intertwined, and peaceful.

When things were not working, it was the world's worst relationship. In those moments, no communication was possible, the squabbling was relentless, and the friction palpable. Times were lighter when the kids were absent because Sophia had no one or no thing to blame. It seemed that she felt the need to challenge my parenting methods. We spent hours processing my modus operandi, creating for us considerable concerns. Despite these battles, we attempted to make a family together.

As her pregnancy progressed, things began to smooth out. The expectation of a baby bound us and we bonded as a family. I was elated to be a father again, which had me begging Sophia for her forgiveness over once wanting to dispose of our child. The kids were excited about the arrival of a baby brother, and they took care of Sophia in ways that supported her pregnancy. When I flew to Israel to be with my mom during surgery for her illness, in my absence, the three of them bonded deeper, with Daniel treating Sophia like a queen. I was filled with love and anticipation, as was Sophia.

About six months into the pregnancy, we had a routine visit with the midwife. On that very day, in a moment of great ardor, we named our baby boy, Aiden. The following day, I took my daughter to the hospital for an x-ray on a previous foot injury. I was in the doctor's office with Talia when Sophia called. There was panic in her voice. Her water had broken and she had started bleeding heavily. Sophia's pregnancy had been tenuous the entire time with much spotting. She had driven herself to a different hospital, so I called a friend to retrieve Talia and rushed from one hospital to the other. Twelve hours later, baby Aiden was delivered—stillborn.

Together, we held our lifeless baby and cried for hours. While cradling Aiden's tiny body—about the size of my hand—I could not stop contemplating the fact that a few months earlier I had wanted to kill him. I had asked the woman, who was the light of my life, to terminate our child. I was engulfed in sadness, regret and guilt, that I had put Sophia through it all. I was haunted by the questions: *Did I create his death? Did my wish somehow come true? Did I kill my son?*

After being discharged from the hospital, we returned a day later for

Sophia to be examined. The doctor spied something in the exam that concerned him, so he ordered an ultrasound. The results revealed that she had sustained internal damage, requiring emergency surgery to prevent the possibility of her bleeding to death. Thankfully, all went well and she recovered fully.

The baby's death was devastating for us all, but if there was a silver lining in this calamity, it was that we became stronger as a family. We healed the best we could, while I was wracked with guilt. I kept asking for Sophia's forgiveness, and although she said she forgave me, I sensed otherwise. I felt a deep resentment and anger lying right beneath her surface, which she seemed oblivious to, so I just carried on.

A few months had passed when Sophia informed me that she wanted to get married. My heart began to race and fear began to rise, choking off all other emotions and feelings. I did not know how to respond, so I tried to stall and placate. Our arrangement was like a marriage any-way—*so why bother, what difference would it make?* But like so many of our issues, marriage quickly became a point of contention. We found ourselves in an ongoing stalemate. All the while, I kept trying to please her to keep her. One day the situation came to a head when we were sitting together in my home office.

"Why don't you want to marry me?" she cried out incredulously. "You're not just anyone, you're the man that I love, the one I'm living with, whose child I carried, whose kids I care for. Why wouldn't you want to marry me? It could only mean that you do not love me."

Sitting next to her, watching the tears stream down her face, I was playing my chess game in my head, trying to conjure up what my next move should be. If she says this, I'll say that. So that's what I did instead of actually relating to her.

"No," I said firmly. "We don't need to get married. What difference would it make anyway? And if we ever did get married, we would need to have a prenuptial agreement."

I would say that was about as far from romantic as one could get.

"Look, you have to make a choice," she said with finality. "If you want to get married, let's get married. If not, I'm leaving. I'm not wasting my time anymore."

The moment she delivered her ultimatum, I felt a sense of panic overcome my entire being. I felt trapped in a discordant state of affairs. That feeling was powerful and painful, yet somehow familiar. It had unearthed something long buried in my psyche.

I loved Sophia but I was afraid to marry her. *Why was I so desperately afraid?* When I searched my head for answers, I saw my previous failed marriage. And then I realized that I did not trust Sophia because she could leave me just as easily as she had left her last boyfriend. I was too afraid to confront her about this, so I brushed my fears aside. I was panic-stricken to get married and equally fearful to not, because she would leave me if I didn't. I had so much dread, I could not envision what I really wanted and actually needed.

All the while, the little voice in my head chatted a never-ending stream of rationalizations why I must not lose her; *you'll be alone...she's wonderful...she's beautiful and young...we shared so many great moments...*

she opened many doors...she healed me...the kids love her. Under that onslaught of rumination, something shifted. I realized that of all my fears, losing Sophia was the greatest, and anything else would be better. I had checkmated myself and surrendered.

"I love you," I declared, "so if you want to get married, we'll get married."

That was how I proposed to Sophia. It was not joyful, tender or particularly loving, but a concession. I was the guy with the proverbial gun to my head, agreeing to a shotgun wedding. In response, she displayed her beautiful face, still wet with tears. She looked relieved, with an expression that I remember as a sense of accomplishment. We made plans to marry in three months.

We met with Sue, a non-denominational and spiritual guide, who was to officiate our wedding. She told us that she felt our connection and that our marriage would be a great journey. Her certainty was inspiring and it left me doubting my fears. Sophia and I swam through an ocean of trauma in losing our baby so I figured that we had a realistic chance at a life together. Maybe being married to Sophia really was the right thing to do. Yes, I did love her, and so I thought—let's roll the dice.

We were married on New Year's Eve in 2010, a date chosen in hopes of signifying a new beginning. Our wedding was unlike any other I had ever attended, held at the spacious home of fellow Landmark graduates, Bob and Bobbie. My kids were in attendance and the ceremony felt very spiritual, warm and intimate. We were surrounded by thirty of our closest friends in a joyous moment. Our wedding day was one of the highest points in our relationship, yet I felt conflicted with a mix of love, hope and fear.

Sophia and I could ill afford a honeymoon nor leave the children, so we plunged into our new life as a married couple. I loved her with the heart of a poet even though I had been confused about marrying her. But I was all in—committed to living with her for the rest of my life

Sophia was the first person that I had ever chosen to love. Loving one's kids is a father's natural instinct but choosing to love a wife is an entirely different narrative. I was a guarded man but she had broken through somehow. She drew me into confiding in her and loving her.

Invitation to Reflect

———

As you can see, I lived in a whirlwind of emotional states. Most times I was operating completely out of fear, and for a few precious moments, living in a space of love.

After that conversation with Hila, my runaway train of fear had stopped and my heart opened, allowing me to see things from Sophia's perspective. I could feel her pain. In that moment, I had found my source of love. In that precise moment, I was free, and life was amazing. Being aware of those precious moments of being love, is a place to come back to, over and over.

I invite you to look at your intimate relationships and connect to them as to whether they originated out of love or fear. This connection comes from self-awareness. Just being aware will connect you to the source. And if you see fear energy sourcing you, share with those intimate relationships how you have been sourcing the relationship from fear. This will present an opportunity to have the fear dissipate, and you can begin to source that relationship from love.

Remember that the significant other in your intimate relationship may be being sourced by fear as well. Allow space for that to be.

Invitation to Reflect
NOTES

Invitation to Reflect
NOTES

_____

_____

_____

_____

_____

_____

_____

_____

_____

_____

_____

_____

_____

_____

_____

Invitation to Reflect
NOTES

_____

_____

_____

_____

_____

_____

_____

_____

_____

_____

_____

_____

_____

_____

_____

Invitation to Reflect
NOTES

_____

_____

_____

_____

_____

_____

_____

_____

_____

_____

_____

_____

_____

_____

_____

_____

CHAPTER 8

DROWNING

As the plane began its descent into Pittsburgh, I steeled myself, knowing things would be difficult when I got home. I just had no idea how difficult. Even though I had a midnight arrival, Sophia insisted on picking me up. And there she was at baggage claim. The sight of her left me feeling awkward, not knowing how affectionate I should be, so I gave her a perfunctory hug. During the drive home, we were mostly silent. There was no animosity or squabbling, but no connection either. The space between us felt unsettled and empty, so we headed straight to bed.

"We have to talk," Sophia said, switching off the light.

"Yes," I replied, "we'll talk tomorrow."

The next morning, instead of sitting down and processing our situation through conversation, she told me she wanted to leave. After losing my mother, this felt like more than I could bear. Nothing I could say seemed to be enough for her to stay. I promised to see a therapist, to try harder, and to get this fixed. I could not sway her. She was resolute and said she would move out the following week. That left little time for fixing.

Meanwhile, life had to go on. We managed to go grocery shopping together. While in the market, we saw a priest whom we both knew. He wheeled his cart over to where we were standing and asked how we were. I replied that I had just lost my mom.

"I'm so sorry to hear that," he said, wanting to be empathetic, putting his hand on my shoulder. "At least you have a wonderful family and a wife who supports you."

Little did he know that my supportive wife was leaving me. I smiled sadly. Inside, I was treading water with no life jacket, barely holding on.

For the next week, I seldom saw my wife. I left for work early and she got home from work late—going to sleep immediately. When together, I continued to persuade her to stay. In response, she barely spoke to me, and her wine drinking increased. Her self-imposed deadline was looming, and so was another. It was time to take my daughter, Talia, to some prospective colleges—a trip that had been planned for months. Again, I felt trapped.

"I have to go, Sophia," I pleaded. "Please be here when we get back. We can work this out, I know we can." She stared at me blankly.

"I'll be gone when you get back," was her response.

"It's just a few days, Sophia, please," I pleaded again.

A few days later, both kids and I piled into the car. If Sophia actually left, I did not want Daniel to be left alone. We toured four schools in five days, driving through a blinding blizzard at one point. It was an epic adventure for Talia—imagining her future education—and I was very proud and excited for her. Even though my heart was breaking, I spoke nothing of Sophia leaving until we got home. The kids became upset and Talia cried. I knew their sadness was for themselves, and for me, as they knew that my losing Sophia would be horrific.

The minute we pulled up to the curb, I could feel it. The house was empty and Sophia was gone. I don't know how to convey how desolate and hollow our home felt. It seemed so devoid of life, as if even the oxygen had fled.

For the kids' sake, I wanted to keep everything as routine as possible. I sent them to their rooms to unpack with the promise of dinner. They scattered quickly and I opened the door to the refrigerator, hoping the contents were enough to inspire a meal, but my mind was blank. I could not make any sense of whatever was in the fridge or freezer or pantry. I was opening and closing doors repeatedly, hoping I might recognize a protein or a vegetable. All I could think about was how the house felt so lifeless—like my life. Sophia was gone and now mother Malka was too.

It was then that my treading water turned to drowning. Tears raced down my cheeks in a torrent and I crumbled to the floor. There was a glow emanating from the still-open door of the refrigerator, its feeble spotlight illuminating my disintegrated corpse. I lay there in a heap—sobbing—with the enormity of what had happened overwhelming me. It was unfathomable, losing the two most important women in my life within days. It was all too much, more than I could handle. And that lifeline, that safety net, my connection to love and all the light in the world—my mother—was gone.

Finally, I gathered myself from the floor and put together some kind of meal. I struggled to put on a mask of normalcy while we ate dinner in silence. Then we went to bed, each of us to our own space of solitude. As I tossed and turned in bed into the wee hours, I kept playing the drama of my life over and over in my mind, looking for where I'd gone wrong, trying frantically to identify the miscalculations that had sealed my fate. Sophia's leaving was my fault—it had to be.

The next day, I had to do what needed doing. I had my kids and a business to be responsible for, but there was a pale over everything. It was more than difficult, it was insufferable. I remember thinking that if I died, I would be okay with that.

There is a darkness that comes with despair, like a coating of oil— heavy and sticking to everything it touches. Although I had my children, a business partner, and some friends, I felt like I had nothing and no one. I was isolated and lost, lacking my usual confidante, my mom. I feared I would stay that way forever.

The darkness was all enveloping and impenetrable. Thinking of the children gave me the strength to push through. I was determined to protect them so I concealed my suffering and soldiered on. All the while, I was tormented by doubts and questions. As one day slipped into another, the darkness remained and sleep eluded me. Before my mother died, sleep was my survival mechanism. I could fall asleep in a moment—even drifting off in the middle of an argument with Sophia.

But now, if I slept for two or three hours a night, it was a blessing. It was fifteen minutes here, fifteen there, and then I would wake up and think about my mom and wife. Being unable to sleep was torturous.

As the days turned into weeks and months, I tried everything I could think of to arrest the torture of my mind. I swallowed medications and sleeping pills but they sickened me. Then I turned to alcohol to numb the pain. One evening, I drank an entire bottle of wine, but to no avail. Eventually, I tried hot yoga, signing up for evening classes in the hopes of exhausting myself into sleep. It made little difference. Nothing did. I went to work every day, sitting in business meetings completely spaced out, sometimes having no clue what was being discussed or decided. I was broken in every conceivable way. My drowning was complete.

I wanted to die.

Despite all the work that I had done on myself, I found the pain of living too great. Often while driving, I remember thinking—*if an oncoming big rig were to swerve into my lane, I would do nothing to avoid it.* And if not for my kids, maybe I would have. I could not find the desire to live.

I wanted to die.

Invitation to Reflect

Scan your past and present to see what moments you can find where you could not go on any longer, but had to just keep going. No need to pass a judgment or make sense of this situation, just write it down. As painful as that it might be, just write it down. We will look at it in the next chapter.

Invitation to Reflect
NOTES

_____

_____

_____

_____

_____

_____

_____

_____

_____

_____

_____

_____

_____

_____

_____

_____

_____

Invitation to Reflect
NOTES

_____

_____

_____

_____

_____

_____

_____

_____

_____

_____

_____

_____

_____

_____

_____

_____

Invitation to Reflect
NOTES

_____

_____

_____

_____

_____

_____

_____

_____

_____

_____

_____

_____

_____

_____

_____

_____

_____

Invitation to Reflect
NOTES

_____

_____

_____

_____

_____

_____

_____

_____

_____

_____

_____

_____

_____

_____

_____

_____

CHAPTER 9

THE QUESTION

How did I get here?

As I sank helplessly to the metaphorical sea floor, unable to descend any further in life, I presented that profound question to myself: *How did I get here?* I recounted what had transpired in my abysmal existence: my first wife was an addict, my second wife abandoned me, my baby died, I had a chronic illness, and my beloved mother was dead. In summation, my life was a fucking mess.

I thought of turning to drugs or alcohol or both to help me numb the pain, but I knew from Nicole that this road led directly to hell. I did not want to lose my kids, my business, or my friends. I did not know much about my soul, but I knew I did not want to lose it. No, numbing and medicating myself was not the answer.

Everyone I knew was really angry with Sophia on my behalf. I could choose to be angry at her as well, blaming her for my pain. I could tell myself that none of this was my fault and that I was the victim, but something stopped me. What if, instead of going down the path of blame, I chose to take responsibility for something—anything—everything?

What if I had a difficult conversation with myself, embarking upon a path of deep self-inquiry? What might I find on the other side? So I asked myself these questions: *How did I get here? What if I follow this trail of inquiry to wherever it leads? Did I create this accursed life?*

I did not know how I would find the strength, but I made the commitment to inquire. And with that, the trajectory of my life radically altered. I proceeded down the road less traveled, and began the process of connecting my head to my heart, and my heart to my soul. Why I had the wisdom to choose this path, I'm not sure. Maybe I sensed that this was the only way I could survive. Or perhaps I perceived that just surviving was no longer working for my dreadful life. I needed to dig beneath myself to find myself—my authentic self.

I do know that from the moment I posed those arduous questions, doors began to open. Experiences and people came into my life to support me on my journey. They appeared at the perfect moments to give me the next piece of information, the next insight, the next lesson learned, the next step on my path to healing.

Invitation to Reflect

———

I inquired within myself, of everything in my life—without placing blame on anyone, especially on myself. It was just to see where I was at the moment—and it was just an inquiry—with no meaning attached to it. So ask yourself: as to how you got to where you are now. Do not make any answers you might find right or wrong or good or bad. Just ask yourself.

There is a chain of links that brought you here. Look at the individual links and see what you can cull from them—without placing great meaning and significance to them. See what emerges for you naturally in a space of openness. Incorporate all of the moments you wrote down from chapter 8.

Start with the here and now and move backwards. You will begin to see how one link led to another, and what link led to that, and to that one as well. Everything that happened in the past is a reaction from something that happened before it. Eventually, you will find the moment that life began for you—in that moment where you said something to yourself about yourself, and you believed that was the truth. You have been a reaction to that ever since.

Your life does not have to have been falling apart like mine. You could be, and have been, in a much better place than I. But you're still a reaction from that moment, and not even aware of it. And without that awareness, you will lack freedom to freely choose your life.

———

Invitation to Reflect
NOTES

_____

_____

_____

_____

_____

_____

_____

_____

_____

_____

_____

_____

_____

_____

_____

_____

Invitation to Reflect
NOTES

_____

_____

_____

_____

_____

_____

_____

_____

_____

_____

_____

_____

_____

_____

_____

_____

Invitation to Reflect
NOTES

_____

_____

_____

_____

_____

_____

_____

_____

_____

_____

_____

_____

_____

_____

_____

CHAPTER 10

TRAPPED

I was terrified, is a recurring theme in my story. I've said it over and over because it exemplifies my state of being for my entire life. Yet, something told me that the only way to move forward was down, down into the muck and mire of life, where all the things were that I avoided. To look at myself, underneath all the layers of myself, to take some kind of hold of Joel, and what I might discover, was of course... an experiment in terror.

It was 2013, and with my therapist Patricia, I started to explore my earliest childhood experiences and the effect they had on me. We looked at how they shaped my beliefs and assumptions about the world, and my life. I began to screen and process the feelings of terror and feeling trapped.

As I took on this investigation, I was surprised to discover how difficult it was to remember. There were many blank spaces which is often a sign of trauma. When childhood issues would surface, I'd instinctively try to block them. Early on in this process, I resisted a great deal.

"Just stay with that feeling," Patricia advised.

As it is often quoted, that was much easier said than done. I had been repressing my feelings for so long that when they finally arose, they felt overpowering. Patricia was patient and persistent. She knew that I needed to get in touch with my formative years, asking me questions to stimulate me, which stirred my memories. During one particular session of probing, I started feeling cornered and trapped, looking for a way out of the moment. I scanned the room, my eyes never landing on Patricia.

"What are you doing," she probed.

I searched the room for doors and windows that could lead me away from my feelings. And then I saw something familiar about those doors and windows. Patricia asked me what I was feeling and at first I said nothing. She encouraged me to stay with the memory. A few moments later I confessed my anger. My father had locked me out on the balcony, so I could not play with my friends below.

"He wanted me to do something that I could not do," I surrendered.

"What was that?" Patricia asked.

"Read," I said, my voice shaking. And with Patricia's guidance, more of my story unraveled.

I liked living in the city of Rehovot, with its bevy of orange groves. In season, the aroma of citrus wafted up to our fourth-floor apartment. Israel was only about twenty-five years old at the time so everything was new, before trees gave way to new housing that supported immigrants pouring into this young country.

In 1973, I entered first grade with an experience beyond excruciating. The fact was that I could not learn to read or write. I had no idea why but when I looked at a book, the letters jumped all around the page. I tried so hard to still them that it made my eyes hurt. I was terrified that there was something very wrong with me. The worst moments came when the teacher called on me to read aloud. On these occasions, I became extremely stressed, often producing an aching stomach. This malady meant that I could get out of school.

My parents were polar opposites in terms of how they responded to my situation. My mother would defend me and my father gave me scorn. One of the school administrators suggested I be sent to a school for the retarded. Mother Malka was defiant.

"My son is not retarded," she bristled—and she was right.

My mom refused to accept this absurd diagnosis. I just had a learning disorder—dyslexia—a condition not commonly diagnosed at the time. Mom knew something was amiss but her refusal to accept their diagnosis left me feeling safe and protected.

Previously, my teacher had told my parents that I was behind in class because I wasn't working hard enough. That was all my father needed to hear. *Yoel is just lazy,* he probably thought. *He knows how to read. He just needs a firm hand.* Of course, my father never said these things, but that's what my young mind conjured up. My dad had decided that discipline would persuade me to work harder. He would lock me out on the balcony with some books, releasing me when I could prove to him that I had read one. I could hear the laughter of kids below as I stared helplessly at the pages. Searching for a way to escape my dilemma, I was saved by Yudith who had opened a rear room window leading to the balcony.

"Don't worry, Yoel," she whispered, "I'll read the book to you."

I then called out to my father to recite passages from the book that Yudith had just read to me, recalling every detail of a story that I could not read. He appeared quite pleased and proud of himself as a disciplinarian, and I was promptly released from my internment.

As I recounted these memories, Patricia again inquired as to what feelings came up for me. I realized how angry I was at my dad, and that the fear of being trapped on the balcony had never left. Patricia asked if I ever felt trapped now and I was stopped in my tracks.

"Absolutely, yes," I said, a feeling of confinement overcoming me.

Then I had a moment of clarity. I distinguished that when Sophia had given me ultimatums about getting married, and then leaving the marriage as I left for Israel, the experiences were one of being trapped with no way out. I began to see that from the moment on the balcony, I created my way out, and I did so by utilizing manipulation. I could have just told my dad that I was just unable to read, but my fear prevented that. So I created the art of manipulation. And I manipulated my way through life—in school, business, relationships—everywhere.

I had the same experience of being trapped with Nicole, but I did not want to go there. And yet, I knew that it was time to deal with what had transpired with the mother of my children.

Invitation to Reflect

———

Here is an opportunity to take a peek in the past to see where you have felt cornered, insecure or trapped. Let's start with the present. Take a look where you feel this way now. Then slowly slide back through the past and look for earlier and earlier moments until you discover the first one (like I did on the balcony). You may find a feeling of no way out, or surrender to defeat, or giving up. When you find that earliest experience, sit with the feelings and allow them to surface so you can get complete with that earliest experience. This can be done in a moment, or it can take time. The completion experience will be different for everyone and powerful for all.

Invitation to Reflect
NOTES

_____

_____

_____

_____

_____

_____

_____

_____

_____

_____

_____

_____

_____

_____

_____

_____

Invitation to Reflect
NOTES

_____

_____

_____

_____

_____

_____

_____

_____

_____

_____

_____

_____

_____

_____

_____

_____

Invitation to Reflect
NOTES

_____

_____

_____

_____

_____

_____

_____

_____

_____

_____

_____

_____

_____

_____

_____

CHAPTER 11

RIDING THE THUNDERBOLT

Settling in the United States was pure happenstance, as was meeting Nicole. The entire Nicole adventure (some may view it as a misadventure) still amazes me. And since I view my life as a journey—filled with salient lessons—life with Nicole just shows up as having been an opportunity to learn about myself, no matter how painful it might have been. How I came to be with this woman was a long and winding road.

In 1989, as a twenty-two-year old, I moved to the Netherlands to pursue my dream of working with horses, which had been my life's passion since my days in the kibbutz. I loved horses. When I was with them, I loved myself. That is to say that I had a higher view of myself while engaged with these animals. Others viewed me highly for my equine expertise, and I judged myself equally. I was good at what I did and I felt better about who I was. And horses did not care if I could read or write.

In Holland, horse dealers brought these wonderful animals to me for jumping and dressage training. However, earning a living this way was very difficult. The days were horrendously long with the bulk spent on horseback. The joy of my life's passion had eluded me. I was feeling burned out, so when a group of friends from the kibbutz suggested that I join them in Brazil, I jumped at the chance.

In 1990, we traveled through South America for a few months. When my friends left for Israel to enroll in university studies—which frightened me to death—I journeyed on to my birthplace, Argentina. I had family in Buenos Aires and came to live with my Uncle Enrique, my dad's younger brother. I had little memory of him except when he and my Aunt Christina had come to Israel for my bar mitzvah. He was gregarious, quite affable, and full of good humor.

The parents of my uncle and father had emigrated from Poland months before the war. At the time, Poland had the largest Jewish community in the world, but by 1938, it had become dangerous to be a Jew. My grandparents managed to get visas to go to Paraguay but somehow ended up in Argentina, creating a new life in Buenos Aires. This is where my father and uncle were born.

Many of my uncle and dad's family members had been murdered in the war sans one cousin, who had managed to escape to Belgium, where Catholic nuns had hidden her. The stories of those surviving the war and those who did not were a large part of our family conversations. I grew up with these stories of death and survival, which unknowingly had left me fearful. They were, however, a celebration of our resilience.

We were never close to my father's family because long distance phone calls to South America were very expensive and letter writing was a slow means of communication. Despite the distance, my aunt and uncle always communicated much love to me, and welcomed me into their home. It was here that I finally made my confession. It happened one evening, when we three were sitting around talking and sharing experiences. After a while, they began a long discussion about a book they had read. They asked me if I had read it as well, and I nodded yes, pretending of course, as I always did. The conversation continued when suddenly I blurted out,

"I can't read."

They looked at each other and then back at me.

"What do you mean you can't read?" my uncle questioned.

"I just can't," I responded. "I have dyslexia, and I can't read and I can't write." There was a silence for a split second and then I remember my uncle's retort.

"Oh, yeah, yeah," he uttered casually, "I remember your mom and dad saying something about that." And then, without skipping a beat, he resumed the book conversation.

I sat there in amazement of my confession. *Why on earth did I just say that?* Amazingly, I felt no sense of danger in my secret having been revealed. They were the only people in the entire country who knew me so my secret seemed safe. I felt accepted by them no matter who I was, but fear still lingered. It took many years for me to speak freely and openly about my dyslexia.

I loved my aunt and uncle and my somewhat luxurious Argentinian lifestyle. I wanted to settle there so I began working in my uncle's clothing factory. He advised me against planting any roots.

"Argentina is a crazy country with a corrupt government," he offered up. "I would love for you to stay here, but you'll have a better future if you go elsewhere. I got used to it here but I don't want you to do the same."

It was 1991, and I was undecided as to my next destination when my mother called to tell me that she had been invited to my cousin's wedding in New York. She suggested that I join her and then we fly back to Israel together. Given the economic climate in Argentina, returning to Israel seemed to make sense, and spending time in New York could be a great adventure.

I was welcome to stay with my Uncle Jack and Aunt Norma in Staten Island. They opened their hearts to me in a way that I could not have imagined. This presented a wonderful opportunity, so even though the wedding was three months away, I decided to fly to New York as soon as possible.

As I awaited my mother's arrival, I found a job with a carpet-cleaning company and became good friends with the owner, Eddie. I worked hard and by the time my mother arrived, I had saved over $4,000, not believing it was possible to earn that much money in such a short time. Only in America! When my mother returned to Israel, I stayed in New York to seek my fortune.

Things were swimming along until 1993, when Eddie could no longer compete with the competition. He decided to move his business to

Pittsburgh and invited me to join him as his partner. This was a step into the unknown as I had never been to Pittsburgh, nor ever had a business partner, or even considered being in the carpet-cleaning business. Nevertheless, I accepted. Eddie and I were both young and all we wanted to do was make money. But I began to feel that the way we were making money was not good for my soul. We engaged in a fair amount of high-pressure, in-home sales, which worked remarkably well. So I buried any ethical thoughts because the lure of good money was just too tempting. Eventually, we considered a business consultant to further our cause. And that is when Nicole walked in the door.

Nicole, a stunning woman with a gorgeous smile, came to our office to sell us consulting services. She was smart, vivacious, well-informed, and could talk to anyone about anything. It was not surprising that she was great at sales and had won our business. Soon, she had won me too.

We started dating and it was great fun being with her, talking for hours. I began to develop a connection to a city I had not previously known. As we grew, her family was very kind to me, which made me feel part of something. Through Nicole, this city was beginning to turn into a home.

Some months later, Eddie had some family issues and was restless to get back to The Apple, and invited me to join him. I chose to stay in Pittsburgh. I say chose, but I'm not sure how freely I chose. I think in some ways I was already beginning to feel trapped.

Looking back, I think I sensed that something might be off with Nicole but I could never put my finger on it. I knew she drank, often to excess, but I dismissed it. It was not until we moved in together that I discovered that she could not control her use of alcohol or drugs.

The first clue came when we began to discuss money for household expenses. She earned good money but was always broke. When I asked why, she was evasive. I knew nothing about substance abuse. I was so naïve and clueless about the grip and power of addiction. The message I got growing up with my mother was that only bad people from bad neighborhoods were alcoholics and junkies. I thought addicts were easily identifiable. I had no idea that someone like Nicole could have an addiction. She didn't hang out on street corners or hole up in crack houses. It took me quite some time to notice some serious problems. But by then they were my problems too.

I knew in my head and my heart that something wasn't right, that I should get out—but I couldn't. I was simply too afraid. The fear for me was abandonment—something that I would soon discover had been a theme throughout my life. Not only did I fear being left, but I feared leaving another. And when I experienced that, I saw my mother and father.

In 1987, my parents had moved from the kibbutz, when my dad tearfully confessed that he had stolen money from his employer. His justification was for a better life for us outside the kibbutz. I asked my mom why she would stay with a thief and her reply was that she could not leave my dad when he was down. And like my father, Nicole was down too, wallowing in addiction. Abandoning Nicole now would have been the same as her abandoning me—and she was all I had. And soon enough there was more—Nicole became pregnant.

I did not want to have a child with her but I felt cornered, so I surrendered to defeat. This was not the woman for me, but I accepted my fate. I would tell myself: *I can fix this, I'll be good for her, and she'll get clean for me, and for the baby.* I watched over her carefully throughout her pregnancy, and as far as I could determine, she had stayed clean. That was a tremendous relief for me—given my concern for the health of our child—and a sign that Nicole was on the road to recovery.

When our sweet daughter was born in 1995, I fell in love with her immediately. We named her Talia. To my great relief, Talia was born with no apparent damage from her mother's alcohol and drug abuse.

For a short time, things were almost good and I had much hope for our future. I opened another carpet cleaning company, operated from our home, so that Nicole could manage the office, and take care of Talia—a nearly perfect situation. Nearly. Soon things turned south. My days were long, my work was hard, and our finances were tight. Then money went missing from the business.

The majority of my business transactions were in cash, leaving substantial amounts of money in the house. At first, I had no clue as to how the money could just disappear. After driving myself crazy, I realized that Nicole was stealing it. I constantly changed the hiding spot but that astute woman would find it eventually. In time, things around the house began to disappear. When I inquired as to their whereabouts, my wife had a story. In fact, she had stories for every inquiry I ever made. It seemed that things of value would simply vanish.

I discovered that when addicts stop using and then relapse, they indulge in their habit with full force. From the moment my wife relapsed, she was wildly out of control, doing both cocaine and alcohol. An addict's life is a series of extremes—racing from high peaks to deep valleys—akin to riding the Thunderbolt at Kennywood Park. Like my experience on that iconic Pittsburgh roller coaster, I was whipped back and forth, unable to get off.

Inside my mind, there was that voice saying—*get off and get out.* Then I heard—*you can't leave. What kind of person leaves somebody who's in such need? How could you do that?* And then there was that trite dialogue—*someday, when she's healthy, I will leave.*

Periodically, she would go to rehab. When she came back, everything would be fine—for a time. When she was clean, being with her was amazing. I would feel hopeful that things would improve. But then, without warning, she would disappear.

One evening, Nicole said she was going out to rent a movie at Blockbuster. I expected her back within the hour, but she was gone for three days. With Nicole missing and no communication, I was frantic. When she came back, I wanted to kill her.

"Where were you?" I demanded, as if that mattered. She spouted excuses.

I knew she was lying but I never challenged her stories, and we fell right back into our Thunderbolt relationship. All the while, I was so embarrassed about my life, I kept Nicole's addiction a secret, even from my own family. I was ashamed of the choices I had made but powerless to make new ones—so the roller coaster continued.

In 1997, Nicole was pregnant again. This time, she proposed that we get married. Her logic suggested that since we were having two children together and were already a family, what is the difference? The contemplation of marriage should have been joyful. Instead, I calculated the risk. On the one hand, I was afraid of what might happen if we married. Our history didn't bode well. On the other hand, nothing was likely to surprise me as I had already seen so much of Nicole's shit. And she had remained sober during the pregnancy, and things had been good between us at that moment. Since I had no Pittsburgh family and had grown to depend on hers, the "we were already a family" logic made sense. So yeah, what was the difference?

We had a small and simple wedding at the local magistrate, then it was off to a nearby restaurant for dinner with her family and friends. Life was really wonderful, for several months anyway. We welcomed little Daniel into our family the next year and all was blissful—until Nicole relapsed, and went completely out of control.

My life had been reduced to reactions, triggered by the needs of my children, the demands of my business, and especially the uncertainty of my wife. I felt trapped, like I was on the balcony in Rehovot. She would act, and I would react. I could have just stopped reacting and leave (which would have been a reaction in itself), but I was in the muck way too deep.

One reaction was to open a safe deposit box because she was stealing money from the house and the checking account. One day I went to the bank to make a routine deposit and the teller commented that she had seen my wife in the vault that morning. Before I could begin to speak, a wave of anxiety and fear engulfed me. I knew that some manner of trouble lay before me. I asked the teller what had brought my wife to the bank.

"She had to put something in the safe deposit box," was the reply.

I was devastated. I knew the money would be gone before opening the box, which I did on the spot. My worst nightmare was realized. I confronted the teller and the bank manager as to how they could give my wife unauthorized access to my box. I suppressed my anger at the bank manager's lack of accountability. He told me that they were sorry for their mistake but there was nothing that they could do. They insisted that I would have to file a report with the police, but I insisted that *they* were responsible for my nightmare. I consulted with an attorney about filing suit against the bank. He reminded me that I was an idiot for not filing a police report against my wife—and he was right—but I just couldn't turn my wife over to the law. Without the report, there was no way to proceed with a suit.

In truth, Nicole was already on probation for a past incident, and if I reported her to the law, she may have gone to jail. In my angered state, I could not have cared less, but in my calmer moments, I just couldn't put her through that kind of hell.

Then Nicole left the house. I wanted to say good riddance, but I was still terrified to leave her and I was petrified to be alone. This was a never-ending trap. It was easier for me to stay and be a victim than to be responsible for having a sane and healthy life. Somehow, it was a comfort to be with someone so damaged because then I could point my finger over there. It was easy to gather evidence that the problem was with my broken wife.

A few days later, Nicole walked in the door with apologies and promises of rehabilitation, and the same stories that I had heard before. I'm sure I asked her where she had been, but I never got a straight answer. And I'm not sure I wanted to hear one. I was happy to see her alive but also wanted to kill her.

One evening, I walked into our kitchen and saw her sitting at the table pumping breast milk.

"What are you up to?" I asked.

"Nothing," she said flatly. "Just pumping milk."

"Why? Are you going somewhere?" I inquired.

"No, I'm just pumping some milk," she countered indifferently.

When she would not look at me, I knew something wasn't right. We went back and forth as I tried to figure out what she was up to. She continued to deny that anything was off kilter. Since we were getting angry, I finally asked her the direct question I was afraid to pose.

"Why aren't you just breastfeeding Daniel?" I continued.

"I don't want to breastfeed anymore," she said softly. "I'm using." At last I had some clarity. She would never stop—ever.

"You need to leave," I demanded. "You can't stay here with the kids if you're using."

Mercifully, Nicole left the house that night. Over time, we would separate and then get back together. Sometimes she would go to rehab, but after a few weeks or months, she would relapse and we would re-collapse. I made every effort to create a stable home life for the kids, hoping to compensate for Nicole's erratic being. Sometimes she would show up unannounced—high of course—and calling the police was the only way I could get her to leave. I had yet to grasp that I was dealing with a powerful disease that owned a powerless woman. It took one last incident to drive that home.

My sister Hila was visiting us from Israel. Late one night, Nicole suddenly walked into the house without knocking and surprised me in the kitchen.

"What are you doing here?" I challenged her after my initial shock. She was obviously wasted.

"This is my house, this is my family, and these are my kids," she rationalized. "I want to stay here."

"You're not going to stay," was my stand. I was afraid of what she might do, so I immediately blocked the stairway leading to our kids sleeping on the second floor. She made it clear she wasn't going to leave.

"If you stay, I'm taking the kids and leaving," I warned.

Nicole refused to leave. In high-action mode, I called out to Hila to help me. While she went to get the car, I ran upstairs, scooped baby Daniel into my arms and carried him outside to my sister. Then I went back for Talia but Nicole already was holding my three-year-old daughter.

"You're not taking her," screamed my wife. But nothing could stop me as I ripped Talia from her arms.

"We're leaving," I roared. As I carried my still groggy daughter down the stairs, she started screaming. Her soul no doubt remembers the ugliness of that night.

With both kids and Hila in the car, and my heart racing like a wild-fire, I realized I had no idea where to go. Then it occurred to me that Nicole would call the police and say that I had kidnapped the children. In fact, she was probably on the phone with the police at that very moment. I saw that my only recourse was to go to the police myself.

I went to the nearby No. 6 police station and gave my name to the desk sergeant, who turned and told someone in a back room that I was there. I was right. Nicole was on the phone telling another officer her version of the story.

"This is what happened," I said to the officer, recounting the events of the last hour. "I came here so that you would know that I am not abducting my children. I just want you to know that the kids are in my car and they're fine. Now if it's okay with you, I'm going to find someplace where we can get some sleep."

The police saw no issues with that, so I drove to the closest motel that I could find.

"I'm sorry," Nicole said the next morning by phone. "I don't know what happened last night, but I'm leaving the house now."

When I returned home with my kids and sister, we found the house torn apart, as if the feds had gone through looking for weapons. Any cash in the house had vanished.

Eventually, I filed for divorce and started the long process of extricating myself from this woman and this turmoil—which took years.

There were further incidents through the years, such as her breaking into our house. I could hear her in the basement attempting to get upstairs but she was unable to breach the door. She would call my name through the door to let her in. All I could do was listen in silence as I was filled with empathetic sadness, along with anger. She was homeless for a time, as she no longer was part of my business and held no job—and any money she had, had gone to her addiction. She would just sleep in the basement.

Finally, about five years after Daniel was born, our difficult and traumatic divorce became final. Through the divorce proceedings, Nicole had partial custody of the kids. She knew she was not capable of caring for them, and for that I give her credit. She did that out of her love for them. She had a legal right to see them, of course, and I agreed, as long as she wasn't using. Nicole was a great mother when she was clean and sober, but when using, it was a completely different story.

Each time she made plans to take the kids, Talia would wait by the door holding her little blue suitcase. Whenever Nicole was a no-show, it tore the kid's hearts apart—and mine as well. After two or three of these disappointments, I stopped telling Talia and Daniel in advance that their mother was coming. I thought they were better off surprised than disappointed.

I had learned a great deal about addiction in the years that Nicole and I were together. I went to multiple AA and NA meetings with her. That's when I learned that she had started to drink when she was nine years old, because tragedy had befallen her. It was something that should never happen to anyone, let alone a vulnerable little girl. At last I had some sense of the depths of her trauma. It did not excuse anything, but it made her behavior understandable and helped me to forgive her. My heart still goes out for her. I hope that one day she will find peace and be able to live life free of substance abuse, and enjoy the simple precious things that life has to offer.

I also attended many Al-Anon meetings in the hopes of discovering answers to my questions: *why did I fill up my life with her problems, why couldn't I leave, and why had I felt so responsible to fix her?* At the time, definitive answers eluded me. I tried to put the entire history of us behind me and move on, but to no avail. I was free of her but not free of my emotional state because I was not yet complete with it all somehow. I could not see the part that I had played—that of being a victim and not being responsible for anything. I thought that I was just with the wrong woman.

Invitation to Reflect

Look at your life and see when you took on living in unmanageable sit-uations. It could be living with an addict, or caring for somebody whose life is unmanageable. You may have been born into a dysfunctional family, have issues with a coworker, a friendship, or it could be you who is experiencing suffering, and feel yourself losing empowerment.

Whichever it may be, look at the part you are playing in it, and find what you are gaining and losing. Be aware of the energy that is sourc-ing you. Are you a reaction from the energy of fear, or are you choosing from the energy of love?

Invitation to Reflect
NOTES

_____

_____

_____

_____

_____

_____

_____

_____

_____

_____

_____

_____

_____

_____

_____

_____

_____

_____

_____

_____

_____

_____

_____

_____

_____

_____

_____

_____

_____

_____

Invitation to Reflect
NOTES

_____

_____

_____

_____

_____

_____

_____

_____

_____

_____

_____

_____

_____

_____

_____

_____

_____

Invitation to Reflect
NOTES

_____

_____

_____

_____

_____

_____

_____

_____

_____

_____

_____

_____

_____

_____

CHAPTER 12

A GIFT FROM MY FATHER

While working with Patricia, I saw the connection of being trapped and living a life of terror, and how my relationships had played out with Nicole and Sophia. I could see the link and the consequences in it all, but was powerless in the face of it. At that point, I was still crazy with pain over my mom and Sophia.

Sophia's office was just a half-block from the house and every time I drove past, it nearly killed me. I just had to get her back to stop the terrible ache in my heart. I tried everything I could think of, such as writing her letters and leaving flowers at her office door. She never responded. She did not want to see or talk to me.

There was a store nearby that she favored, and out of desperation, I went to buy her something special in the hopes of winning her over. I had become acquainted with the saleswoman and we would make small talk while I wandered about looking for the perfect gift. She often spoke in glowing terms about a man named Carlos who worked in the office upstairs.

"Who is Carlos?" I inquired. "You always speak so highly of him."

She said he was a very gifted tarot card reader. I was curious about tarot and knew it had something to do with tapping into the unknown, which to me meant messing with the universe. That idea scared the hell out of me, but I was ready to grasp at anything that might bring some light into the darkness. Either I had suddenly become courageous, or was so broken that I didn't care.

I made an appointment with Carlos who turned out to be quite colorful, sporting multiple rings on his hands and necklaces draping his torso. Originally from Puerto Rico, he was extremely talkative and had a powerful and infectious laugh. Before I knew what was happening, he was chattering on about energies and angels, and how the stars were doing this and that. I didn't understand a word of his diatribe, and my first impression was that he was way too spiritual for me. It was instantly apparent that he was not merely gregarious but deeply kind and sensitive. I liked him immediately and before too long, he became my good friend.

To begin the session, we sat down at a table and he was shuffling a strange-looking deck of cards. Before the reading, he described how he worked.

"I become the cards," he said.

He laid the cards face down in a strange formation. While turning over each card, he shared with me what he saw. Everything was there, a map of my life thus far. He talked about someone dying and someone leaving, both of them female. He spoke about my business, and toward the end, he described my troubled relationship with my dad who had passed away a few years earlier.

After interpreting the cards, Carlos sat back and inquired as to my experience. I told him I was amazed. How did he know all of this stuff? Then I shared that my mom had just passed and my wife had recently left. I had hoped that we might reunite.

"Your wife is gone," he said, looking at me with a firm gaze.

"You can't know that," I responded. I knew that he meant gone permanently, but I didn't want to believe him. But Carlos just pointed to the card that represented Sophia.

"See," he said, "her back is to you and this card is from the arcana of spears, or knives. It means the relationship is cut. She's gone. The cards say it will not work."

I resisted this notion. I was the fixer and I could find a way to win her back. Then he said my mom was watching over me. I don't know if he saw this in the cards or it was just intuition, but it didn't matter. I had always felt that she was there somehow, but in that moment, he made it real. I knew then that my mom was not completely gone and it was tremendously comforting to know she would always be there.

"Your dad is trying to communicate with you," he told me unexpectedly, as we were wrapping up our session. "He has a message for you" I was incredulous.

"I barely talked to my dad when he was alive," I said. "Now he's dead and he wants to talk?"

"All I know is that this is what the cards say," replied Carlos. "My advice is to just be open to it."

I thought with skepticism that I would try to be open, but it was not like I was anticipating hearing from my father.

Shortly after seeing Carlos, I ventured again into the unknown. I had been having such a hard time sleeping and I was beyond desperate. I did some online research, looking for alternative ways to deal with my insomnia. The first thing I found was acupuncture, so I made an appointment with a practitioner named Peter. For several weeks, I worked with this diminutive man in his late thirties who emanated ease and healing. In one particular session, Peter inserted some needles into my body and left me alone to relax. When he returned, he asked how I was feeling. It would have taken me ten hours to tell him everything in my head in the last ten minutes. I could make no response or gesture. I was overwhelmed.

"So, in other words, this is no fun," he chuckled. "Let's try something else."

Peter inserted needles into my ears and forehead and shut off the lights. Within seconds, the goings-on in my head disappeared as I entered a state of deep relaxation. It was then that I saw my father. The vision, if that's what to call it, was quite vivid. I saw him from the waist up in a background of light, with blue sky and various colors surrounding him. And then we communicated. I'm not sure how long this experience lasted. Perhaps it was a split second or maybe ten minutes, as there was no real sense of time. I don't think I ever heard his voice exactly and I'm not sure that he ever heard mine, but we were definitely communicating. It was a short conversation and a complete out-of-body occurrence. I was in awe and felt enlightened. Then I uttered an unexpected confession.

"I am sorry I abandoned you," I told him.

"I know," was his reply.

When I tried to continue using my conscious mind, the communication ended and he disappeared, leaving me yearning to stay connected. When Peter came back, he asked about this last experience. I told him I was embarrassed to say because he would think I was crazy. But I confessed anyway that I had seen my father. I shared some background on how the communication between my father and me had deteriorated after my parents' divorce.

During my early twenties while living in the States, there were times when I flew to Israel to visit my mom and sisters but never stopped to see him. As a young child, I knew that my parents did not have a good relationship. Even before the incident of my dad stealing money, my mother could not tolerate him. In response, dad would isolate himself, sitting in the living room for hours reading the newspaper. As a father, he should have been responsible for keeping the family together. Instead, he distanced himself, which angered me. Many years after their divorce, I felt loyal to my mom, but that did not require me to completely abandon my dad.

Peter appreciated me sharing my background with him and as I left, I felt exhilarated but confused. For weeks, I battled with my dad's words, "I know." I took those words to mean that he knew I was sorry.

I wanted him to say, *I forgive you,* but he didn't. *Why didn't he just say that he forgave me?* I didn't even know why I had said I was sorry. The more I thought about it, the angrier I became. *It wasn't enough that I was angry at you while you were alive,* I thought, *but now you're dead and I said I'm sorry, and you can't even say I forgive you?* In the midst of my anger, I remembered something that Carlos said in a reading.

"Your dad is trying to teach you a lesson," he declared.

My anger shifted to curiosity. What could this lesson be? I started to inquire as to why my dad had not said, I forgive you. I started to investigate why I had said "I'm sorry I abandoned you." This word, abandonment, was not part of my vocabulary. I had no reference to it, given that English is my second language. I didn't even know how to pronounce it. But this word, abandonment, had lingered in my mind, festering in the background, and eventually would source every part of my entire life.

Once the word entered my lexicon, I saw the fear that I had surrounding the word abandonment. I had no prior relationship to this word. I saw that I had to deal with it but what do I do with it? Now that it's out, I can't put it back in the bottle, so now I have to face it.

This opportunity was presented by my dad not speaking those words that I thought I wanted to hear. Had my father said *I forgive you,* I would have gladly accepted it and never given it another thought. A gift from my father was indeed, "I know."

Invitation to Reflect

———

Look at your life events that caused you suffering, or made you uncomfortable, angry, defeated, or less than. You might still be dealing with the consequences of these events...physically, emotionally, or both, Wherever you are with this, it's okay, This lesson taught (and hopefully learned) does not mean you did something bad or wrong.

Consider that these events may have happened to teach you a life lesson. Life has a way of teaching us lessons in ways we sometimes (and most often) cannot explain. These lessons are often to be found where life is uncomfortable. This is the area where there are opportunities for you to learn about yourself and grow as a human. And in growth, there is freedom and power.

Often we say to ourselves that we will never do certain things again because we don't want to re-experience some things. And yet, we continue to do the same things over and over because we are continually reacting from fear, which is the basis of survival mode, established at an early age. Then we do the same things again but in a different way, yet still sourced from fear. And then we put up safeguards, like our eggshells. Everything I did in all its various forms, were all sourced from my fear of abandonment.

Reshape your experience of past events by looking at them through a new lens—the lens of love, compassion, kindness and understanding. Complete the fear energy of the experience that is still shaping your life by bringing much love, compassion, kindness and understanding to yourself. This will have a profound impact on your relationship with others as well.

———

_____

_____

_____

_____

_____

_____

_____

_____

_____

_____

_____

_____

_____

_____

_____

Invitation to Reflect
NOTES

_____

_____

_____

_____

_____

_____

_____

_____

_____

_____

_____

_____

_____

_____

_____

_____

CHAPTER 13

FINDING ANGELS

After my positive experiences with Carlos and Peter, I began seeking out others for support. The acupuncture sessions helped me sleep, which replenished me. The more sleep I received, the more power my mind and body had. And with that, things began to calm down and shift. I began searching for an answer to that question: *how did I get here?*

In the weeks that followed, I heard about a woman, Nora, who facilitated past life regressions. I wanted to pose the question: *how did I get here?* Intuitively, this conversation felt like the next step. I talked to Nora for maybe two minutes over the phone and I knew she was the right fit.

"Don't tell me anything more about you," I said, and made the appointment immediately.

Nora was a sweetheart. She was small with blonde hair and a warm smile, and a loving presence. Eventually we became friends, having intimate conversations about our lives. Throughout these conversations, there was an even balance between the spirit of the past life and this one, with a peace and acceptance of the life in which we were now living.

The first session was all about abandonment. Nora said that my experience of being repeatedly abandoned throughout my many lifetimes had been so traumatic, that I would do anything to prevent the experience from repeating. I did not fully understand what this meant but I did have an experience of her being authentic in her expression of it. Then we did an exercise that cleared this emotional weight from my life. At her direction, I recited a short prayer—a mantra of sorts— three times a day for a month. Even this was a stretch for me because prayer was out of my comfort zone, as was the entire concept of a past life. I was new to disciplines such as therapy, energy work, and spirituality.

It had been about five months since my mother passed away and Sophia had left. In just a short period of time, I had done a tremendous amount of experiential inquiry, but had not experienced healing in either my body or mind. In fact, great anxiety had set in, as Talia and Daniel were about to leave home simultaneously.

Talia was heading to Haiti, volunteering in the recovery efforts of a recent earthquake. Daniel was off to basketball camp. The moment they left, I saw that I was terrified of being alone. My kids were my lifeline, and without them, the void was alarming and threatened to swallow me. In a panic, I bought a ticket to Israel and justified the trip as a need to complete my mother's estate. Over there were the people who loved and accepted me, and I needed that more than oxygen. One of them was Dalya, whom I called when I arrived.

Dalya was ten years older than I and had been in my life since I was a child in the kibbutz. She was the caregiver for our class, making sure that we were fed and clothed. Tall with long black hair and an aura of confidence and love, she took me under her wing, becoming my private tutor. She guided me throughout my teenage years and supported me in a project that was very dear to my heart—the mental disease that horses develop from confinement.

In a presentation of the project to my class, I shared the symptoms that horses display from this condition—the relentless pacing back and forth like a caged lion. I explained that animals never exhibit this kind of behavior in the wild. It is a symptom of their feeling trapped. I earned an "A" for that project, the only "A" I ever received in school. Looking back, I am incredibly moved by my youthful compassion for animals who felt trapped—like horses pacing and a chick in an egg-shell. Given what I now understand about my own history of feeling cornered, this makes sense.

With Dalya, I always felt kindness, love, respect, safety, and acknowl-edged for my talents. With her I could be myself and we connected in a very powerful way. When she left to attend the university to become a teacher, she continued to tutor me. We stayed in touch and from time to time, I would stop to say hello when returning to Israel.

On this trip, she shared with me that she had become an energy healer which intrigued me greatly. We talked at considerable length at her home on the Mediterranean Sea across from the kibbutz. It was a powerful conversation. She had taken a journey from teacher to ener-gy healer—the result of some serious back issues.

Dalya had gone to conventional medical practitioners with limited results, so she started questioning what was the true source of her back problem. She searched for it in the healing powers that connected her to God, to the universe, and to people. I shared with her some of my journey, which was to heal myself of the MS diagnosis. But I had just been doing *the doing*—watching my diet, taking supplements, exercising, and so on. What was missing was *the being* in *being* healthy. I had no spiritual connection so I was new to this path, and I still had some emotional pain and physical limitations.

We walked along the boardwalk by the sea and I told her that I was committed to a life of profound health, and I was not going to stop until this was so. Suddenly, she stopped to ponder a thought.

"What if this is as good as it gets?" she asked softly. "Would you be able to accept that?"

I did not respond because I did not have an answer, and her question triggered a rush of fear throughout my body. Dalya was very soft-spoken but a straight-shooter. She wouldn't say things just to make me feel good, nor hold back if there was something I needed to hear. I knew she was referring to my ever-present limp, but her question referred to so much more. I did not want to even consider the possibility that this was "as good as it gets." This question was literally the last thing I heard her say before parting ways.

When I returned to Pittsburgh, the question she posed played over and over in my mind. *What does this question even mean? Do I surrender to things being the best they can be? Am I powerless?* I contacted her and we agreed to work together, with me being her first global client. And we have a working relationship still today that includes a great friendship and powerful communications.

In my intended state of awakening, I was going to be powerful and walk normally. Not only that, I would overcome the loss of my wife, and find a new one. I had made a good deal of progress in my self-healing and in some of my spiritual awakening, but Dalya's question fed my fears that I would lose my power and return to my automatic way of being—terrified and abandoned. Her question left me feeling that it was inevitable that one day, I would again shut my eyes to my awareness. Although I had a taste of freedom through this awareness, her question hit me like; that is all there is, and will ever be, and I'll never get any further. This will be forever, the way it is today.

I had seen a glimpse of my power and freedom inside of my new-found awareness, so I started an inquiry. What if I can change things, any things, all things? I am powerful, and when I put my mind to something, I can accomplish anything. That's who I am. I am unstop-pable. I've overcome so many challenges in my life. I have no limits. All of this went on in a split of a second, as my mind went from dusk to dawn.

I'm not sure if this is what Dalya meant when she asked me this question, but, what if this is as good that it will be for today? What if I accept and appreciate every little thing that happened in my life? What if I'm so thankful to have in my life what is good and bad for today? Tomorrow will be another day for me to experience life. And what will that bring?

I could now see that accepting life came with all sorts of circumstances. Pain and suffering, and sadness and fear, were as prominent in my life's journey as love and happiness, and joy and contentment. They were all part of the winding path. I accept the things that make me feel bad as readily as the ones that make me feel good. I do not need to be a certain way in life to accept my life. I have the ability to ask this question every day. Every day is a new beginning.

Invitation to Reflect

———

And what if this is "as good as it gets?" What if this is it—all that life has to offer? Can you accept? Can you simply accept life as it is, not having to have it be better or improved in some way? Life is not greener over there.

Reflect on the various areas of your life: physical, emotional, spiritual, financial, and relationships. Look to see where you are stuck, unhappy, unfulfilled, and feeling that there is more to life than just this. There is a tremendous amount of freedom in accepting where we are in our life right now, without having to change, to fix, or to improve.

We can release all the fear energy that is running the show, opening up the possibility for the energy of love to source our lives. By accepting love into our lives, we can create so many wonderful things and be at peace with ourselves, with our surroundings, our circumstances and experiences—having every area of life transform.

Most people view life as having more and better as the key to love and acceptance. Consider that being love and acceptance will lead to what you consider more and better, but is really just you fulfilling on your life's potential.

Invitation to Reflect
NOTES

Invitation to Reflect
NOTES

_____

_____

_____

_____

_____

_____

_____

_____

_____

_____

_____

_____

_____

_____

_____

Invitation to Reflect
NOTES

CHAPTER 14

TOMORROW CAME YESTERDAY AND I MISSED IT

Working with Dalya was incredible. And with her question still lingering in my mind, I continued to expand my journey. When my mom was drawing her last breath, I had this thought—what is the point of this life? Then immediately I thought perhaps I could find some answers in meditation and yoga, which I had been exposed to earlier. Prior to my conversations with Dalya, Nora, and others, spirituality had not been my strong suit. In fact, I had long been convinced that God was a hoax and religion a scam. But I found a great deal of spirituality in meditation.

While I was looking for some answers to my questions, I was also seeking to escape the pain of my life. I joined a meditation class and began to feel more grounded, centered and calm. One day while meditating, two words appeared—kindness and compassion.

The Dalai Lama had spoken about these values and the message seemed to be more kindness and compassion for myself. At first these words seemed so alien that I rejected them out of hand. But as

I looked at my life, I saw that almost every hour of my day was given to others; to my employees, my clients, and surely my kids. Entire months had gone by without me having a single moment of kindness and compassion for myself. *Why couldn't I give myself one single hour? What was I asking here?*

I recall about 15 years ago, I was doing laundry and being unable to fold the clothes because I was depleted of all energy. I had carried the basket up two flights of stairs with my back screaming in pain. I was thinking that; *I must keep sacrificing today—even sacrificing my health for the kids' laundry—for a better tomorrow.* But sadly, tomorrow had already come yesterday and I had missed it. I realize now that all of that sacrifice, that had seemed so necessary, was extremely inauthentic. I was not giving my time to others from a place of love and compassion, but out of shame and low self-worth—a result of a lifetime of fear. And I continued to sacrifice for years.

My greatest sacrifice was the veto of my feelings. Through the years, I repressed them to make it through the day. I felt that I did not have the luxury of feeling anything, so I sacrificed all relationships, spending little time in intimacy or friendship. I felt compelled to do, and do, and accomplish. It was one hurdle after another. Life was all so significant, and my survival mode was in overdrive. The sheer act of survival consumed all of my time and energy—like a fire devouring oxygen—leaving me physically and emotionally depleted. Then I saw how I believed I was not important. But what if I was someone of importance? What would that look like? When I examined that, an entire new world opened up.

I decided to try something radically different. I began treating myself with kindness, compassion, and self-respect every day, making sure that I did something positive and powerful for myself. One day, I made an appointment with my massage therapist. On another, I had some therapy with Patricia. I might have acupuncture from Peter or a reading with Carlos. I might go for a walk or take a yoga class, or meditate. These were all moments just for me.

Then I decided to observe Yom Kippur—the highest of Jewish holidays. The observant is supposed to fast and contemplate one's life, seeking forgiveness everywhere. It is customary to gather with friends and family on the eve of the holiday to enjoy a last meal before fasting. I did not just observe, but hosted a dinner for my closest friends. This was quite an anomaly. It had been many years since I had last observed this holiday, always participating half-heartedly. I might have accepted an invitation from a hosting friend, but I would have never initiated one myself. For me to actually host, prepare, and cook—was extraordinary.

Before the guests arrived, I took some time to sit quietly, becoming present and in the moment. I began thinking about what I wanted to say, and from whom I needed to ask forgiveness. To my surprise, acute discomfort set in. I was taken aback by my experience of myself. *Why was I so uncomfortable?* A spike of fear pierced me. I wanted to cancel the gathering immediately but then I heard in my mind Patricia's voice urging me to stay with the feeling. As I did, something opened up. The person from whom I needed to ask for forgiveness was...myself. As soon as I asked that question, the answer rushed in— *you need to forgive yourself for letting fear control your life.*

I didn't want to ask anyone for their forgiveness when I couldn't even muster forgiveness for myself. But this act of humility was expected as a tradition of the holiday. I felt very inauthentic asking anyone for forgiveness. This powerful affirmation of self-forgiveness, and the divine visit from my dad (which allowed me to be present to abandonment) had jolted me into forgiving myself for letting fear control my life.

In this very moment, I began cracking my eggshell. I was on my own, and I was fracturing my protective crust.

I opened myself to just being vulnerable, raw and exposed. I gave up control and put myself out there in the world, out in life. Suddenly, I was exhilarated. I felt like skydiving without a parachute. There was this experience of weightlessness, freedom and peace of mind.

I also began to understand with increasing clarity the role that the fear of abandonment had played—and all of its implications. My mother's death had shown up as abandonment and so had Sophia's leaving. I could hear the voice of fear when I re-read the letters I had written to my wife: *please don't leave me, I'm dying, just come back, just come back.* This shook up everything I knew about myself. I thought of myself as needing to hide the shameful secret of dyslexia, but the idea that I was terror-stricken of abandonment had never occurred to me until all of this self-inquiry. I saw that the fear had been there as far back as the moment I did not get promoted to the second grade. Then, I had a flashback to the kibbutz.

I was ten years old, staring at the incubator with the little chick trying to peck through its protective shell. It's no wonder that I was so fascinated with this moment because I had spent the first ten days of my life in an incubator, according to my mother. I was a bit premature and had been incubated since birth. *Had I been abandoned for those ten days with no maternal love and connection?* Those thoughts were overpowering.

The ten of us gathered for my Yom Kippur dinner, with none of us particularly devout. With nothing formal planned, I felt an obligation to say something and lead the evening. I stood up at the end of the long table and spoke of the traditions of the holiday. Since I could not read, I just shared something from my heart. I spoke of this day being a day when we ask for forgiveness, but that I felt inauthentic to ask or give such to others, if I didn't forgive myself.

That dinner was the moment I forgave myself for the first time. I declared to the entire dinner table about the paralyzing experience of being in fear mode throughout my life. I was unstoppable in sharing my discovery of the grip that fear had on me. The end result was a physical and emotional release. There was not an absence of fear but an acceptance of it, for what it was—just fear. If I found myself being fearful, I could go back to see when the fear had started running the show. And in those moments, I could go back to the memory of the Yom Kippur dinner and re-experience the exhilarating freedom that I had felt inside of my confession and declaration.

Invitation to Reflect

———

Forgiveness is a powerful virtue. If we don't forgive ourselves for our past, we will never be able to seek forgiveness elsewhere, as the cycle of forgiveness will be incomplete. Once I forgave myself for being paralyzed by fear, my life completely transformed, as I then had this power to transform anything.

Make a list of all the things that you need to ask forgiveness from yourself for, like things you did or didn't do, promises that you made and broke, promises that you never made because you did not have the courage to. Then make a list of all the people you want to ask forgiveness from, and the people you want to forgive—and why.

When you look at the journey that brought you to each place in life, where you see something to forgive, see what energy is there. You will discover that it is most likely fear energy. Be aware of this energy and look it in the eyes. Do not run away from it, just breathe and let it be. The fear energy will lose control over your life once you accept that it is part of your life journey. And when you finally stop reacting from fear, you will find freedom. Forgiving yourself leads to you forgiving others who are also living in a reaction from fear.

Invitation to Reflect
NOTES

_____

_____

_____

_____

_____

_____

_____

_____

_____

_____

_____

_____

_____

_____

_____

Invitation to Reflect
NOTES

_____

_____

_____

_____

_____

_____

_____

_____

_____

_____

_____

_____

_____

_____

_____

_____

_____

Invitation to Reflect
NOTES

_____

_____

_____

_____

_____

_____

_____

_____

_____

_____

_____

_____

_____

_____

_____

_____

Invitation to Reflect
NOTES

CHAPTER 15

ACUTE FEAR

I can see and feel it. Essentially, the entire time I was in school and in the kibbutz, I existed in a state of relentless fear. I was terrified people would discover my secret and think I was stupid. Ironically, in the kibbutz, most of the kids already knew and didn't care that I could not read, but the point was lost on me as a child.

Despite confessing to my aunt and uncle in Argentina, my world had not fallen apart. But I remained stubbornly convinced that if anyone knew of my horrible secret, they would abandon me, just as my parents had. That wasn't true of course—my parents had not abandoned me. We had just moved to the kibbutz out of economic necessity and we were no longer living together. But the combination of the move and my failure to move on to second grade, seemed like a cause and effect.

Even though I carried the burden of being discovered as illiterate, the fear of abandonment had become my greatest horror. That fear had controlled everything. It had dictated every action and every decision I had made, including what relationships I had and what kind of work

I did. All along, I thought I had been making choices, but I was just reacting from fear. For forty years, secrecy and fright had become a daily way of being and living.

I began to see how the fears of being outed about my illiteracy and of abandonment had dominated my intimate relationships. My entire life had been based on these two diabolical fallacies, and they were intricately intertwined.

I would continue the pretense of knowing how to read, even when I suspected my partner knew otherwise. I would go to great lengths to hide the truth, so I was never authentic with anyone for fear of discovery and rejection. Again, I played it like a chess game, anticipating the other's moves (questions) so I could strategize my response. This was exhausting and certainly left no space for intimacy. And I had no idea at the time that my fear of abandonment was even an issue. This was in my blind spot.

In my teens, my first love, Meirav must have known of my inability to read, but it was never mentioned. It never surfaced in other relationships as well. Even Nicole knew, but I never gave the topic any acknowledgement. Convinced that I was stupid, I felt incredibly vulnerable. The only way to feel safe in a relationship was to be with a woman who also had secrets or was broken in some manner—preferably someone with more harrowing and menacing issues than mine—a woman even more vulnerable than myself.

I had long been haunted by the question of why had I chosen Nicole. I began to understand. I chose her because I knew she had been traumatized. Being in a relationship with an addict made me feel valuable and needed. Because her life was so insane, it kept the focus away from me. Her addiction afforded me a kind of safety, as it was very unlikely that Nicole could ever better me in any way, so I would always have more power. I questioned why I had stayed put when her life (and mine) had spun out of control. Why did I keep putting up with the abuse, lying and stealing? The fear of abandonment so controlled my life that I had to be loyal at any cost. Suddenly, I saw a connection to my parents' relationship. The answer pointed to my dad.

My mom and dad had major problems in their marriage but remained together. Whenever I asked my mother why she stayed, her reasoning was that she couldn't leave because my dad was in some crisis or other difficult situation. She would say that he needs to be stronger before she could leave him. I saw how that message had lodged itself in my psyche—that you can't leave someone when they're down. While that may have been honorable, my decision to stay with Nicole did not come from compassion, but from intense fear of being alone. I might have stayed with her longer than I had, if not for the safety of my kids.

After Nicole, there was Sophia. In the beginning of our relationship, she wanted to text but I told her that texting was not personal. At some point I felt safe enough with her to share my secret. I kept nothing from her unless I was unaware of it, which turns out to be quite a bit. She was the first person of an intimate relationship that I was completely open with around my dyslexia.

Again, the fear of being alone was so overwhelming that I acquiesced to Sophia's ultimatum about getting married. I was with her because I loved her, but that love was based in fear, not on a solid foundation— not enough to keep our marriage together. But what if instead of focusing on the secrets, I had been present to the love? My fears were an interference to the love that we had for each other.

I had not learned any lessons from the failure of my marriage to Nicole, so I had to have a failed second one. Sometimes one lesson is not enough and sometimes we never learn.

Even my motivation to have my own business was rooted in fear. So I created a mini-empire of small businesses because working for someone who might ask me to read was just too risky. Moreover, I wanted to run my own businesses to prove to the world—and myself—that I was not stupid. We often try to prove to ourselves that we are *not* what we are afraid we are.

Invitation to Reflect

The willingness to be vulnerable is the access to freedom. This is one of my most powerful affirmations that I can share with you. Being vulnerable may look like weakness, but what is at play here is a fear of looking weak. To be vulnerable is actually courageous, not weak. It takes great courage to show one's vulnerabilities. Putting yourself on the line like that is acting in the face of fear. And one way to show one's vulnerability, is to share your darkest secrets.

We all carry secrets, large and small. Some are responses to events that impacted us, and some are completely fabricated in our minds (like my fear of abandonment). By being willing to be vulnerable, you can share those secrets, allowing you to complete energetically, with the secrets that constrain you. There is much freedom to be gained in this.

As an exercise, write down all of the secrets you carry with you. This is not an easy exercise and will take courage...and vulnerability. There is a tremendous weight on your mind, body and soul, in toting these secrets around through life. There is freedom, peace and joy on the other side of secrets and fear.

Look for the fear and terror that you live in around these secrets. How terrified are you in living inside of the eggshell? Acknowledge the fear and accept it as part of the journey. No need to resist it, although you will automatically work hard to do just that. That's the survival mechanism kicking in. The fear loses its power once you accept the fear as part of life. This exercise in courage and vulnerability can be priceless.

Invitation to Reflect
NOTES

Invitation to Reflect
NOTES

_____

_____

_____

_____

_____

_____

_____

_____

_____

_____

_____

_____

_____

_____

_____

_____

Invitation to Reflect
NOTES

_____

_____

_____

_____

_____

_____

_____

_____

_____

_____

_____

_____

_____

_____

_____

CHAPTER 16

THE MOMENT

Even though I had some insights and experienced some calm and clarity through meditation, I was still tormented by Sophia's leaving, and still fantasized about her return. Though she had cut off all communication, I finally got through to her and she agreed to meet to discuss our divorce—the thought of which hit me straight in the gut. I saw an opportunity to convince her otherwise by charming her and sharing everything I learned about myself and my life.

We met at a restaurant in Highland Park called Point Brugge Cafe, talking for hours about everything except the subject of dissolving our marriage. I was thrilled with the lack of divorce talk, and she seemed light and free. It reminded me of when we were dating. After dinner, we walked to my car to get her some things that I had brought from the house.

"Why are you being so nice to me?" she asked suspiciously.

"Because I love you," was my obvious answer. We hugged and said goodbye, and agreed to talk the next day.

The next day, I was floating. My fears of being alone and abandoned had disappeared, leaving me hopeful and happy. I felt safe now, and would not have to fight so intently inside myself. I was optimistic for the future, and for our family.

A few hours later, she called and told me that she loved me and always would, but that she had not been honest at Brugge. She confessed that she was involved with another man. In a second, I went from cloud nine to the bottom of the Grand Canyon. It was an unmitigated and excruciating crash.

I was already starving for affection, intimacy and peace, and found myself once again in deep survival mode. There was exhaustion from the struggle, confusion, and loneliness. Afraid that I could not overcome my pain fast enough, I craved for someone to rescue and fix me. I was in need of a volcanic event in my life.

In my darkness and despair, I was transported once more back to that moment in the kibbutz, with the chick trying so desperately to peck its way to freedom. No sooner had I recognized this scene, when suddenly, I was no longer merely watching the chick—I was the chick—inside that dark and confining shell, yearning to break through. There I was, flailing, terrified, exhausted, and defeated. It seemed like the chick (me) was silently begging for someone—anyone—to come to the rescue, like Yudith had done on our balcony so long ago. Then I heard a voice in my mind. It was Yaov emphatically admonishing,

"No! The chick has to do it by himself," he commanded, "to develop the strength he needs for life."

I sat with *this moment* for a very long time, realizing that my chick needed to break through that thin but tenacious crust. I had options, but only three that I could see: remain in my shell and live in the deep fear and pain in which I had been wallowing; hope to find an intimate relationship to ease my pain (which would help open the shell for me); or bust through the eggshell on my own and see what was on the other side. That was *the moment—the moment* I chose to bust through the eggshell. In *that moment—that moment* of pure clarity—I found my profound relationship to life.

In *the moment*, I saw the impact of living a life in total fear. In the *moment*, I saw that I could start living life as a journey, and not as a destination. Yes, that was *the moment*—and it bears repeating—it was *the moment* life became a journey, and not a destination.

I had been living my life as a destination, as some place to where I needed to get. Wherever I was, was not good enough. There was never peace wherever I was. It was a life unfulfilled and unsatisfied. In living a life of destination, there is no room for mistakes. It is just winning or losing, with every step calculated. When living a life as a journey, what was once a mistake or failure, can become an opportunity for growth and freedom. In fact, you could consider that there are no mistakes in the journey, only learning opportunities and life lessons. Only when I got to that realization could I accept the past, and then expand from my life experiences.

I had no real choices in life until *the moment*. What had been occurring as choices were actually reactions from fear. It was pure survival, as in do-or-die. Everything was so meaningful and significant. (When I speak of significant, I speak to how ultra-important things became, but in a constraining way). I saw that I could accept myself for who I am, in *the moment*, and not get caught up in the stories I had of myself. Newly, peace and spirituality had emerged.

In *the moment*, I had an out-of-body experience, a sort of universal face-slap, a God-like second that led me to gain the courage to break through. The chick doesn't have a choice in breaking through—it is innate—it is time. *The moment* was my time.

Now I could traverse from survival to opportunities. What did life have to offer from a place of freedom and love that is contained inside of opportunities, and not from safety and fear that is the basis of survival? This was another profound moment in my awakening. Now nothing was as significant as it had been. Inside the eggshell, every little step or instance carried great weight. Every moment had to be controlled so that it all worked out and the goal was achieved, arriving at the proper destination.

It became clear that remaining in my shell would keep me safe, but living small and fearful. The shell had grown so tight, so confining, it was killing me, slowly and steadily. I had thoughts of dying because I was. When I got complete with that realization, life came alive. It was like a fever had broken. I was drenched in sweat and weak as a kitten, but I felt sublime. In *the moment*, I had gotten the impact of "*The Eggshell Effect.*"

I went into the unknown with blind faith, sensing what the next step might be. I felt that the access to freedom was to tell *my* truth and be vulnerable, in order to break through the shell. I needed to tell the truth about myself and share all of my secrets, as I had accumulated so many while in the practice of keeping them. Even larger—I could share my emotions and pain, which previously had been impossible. I no longer needed to live a life so guarded.

After this revelation, I started to let go of everything I had made significant. Bit by bit, I began trusting in something larger than myself—like the energy of humankind, or God, or the Universe. I began trusting in the journey. I was astounded by the volume of fear energy that I had carried, and how much manipulation I thought was necessary to feel safe. I was so invested in keeping all of my secrets. I had lived a double life, not realizing how it had cut me off from the love and caring of people around me—and most of all, from myself.

For the first time in my life, I let myself be completely vulnerable and authentic, which was quite frightening. Today, I tell people that the moment I stopped letting fear run me, when I let my guard down, when I became vulnerable, when I told the truth—that's *the moment* when my life truly began.

It's the awareness of the fear that makes the difference. I can now choose to be with fear, with all of its thoughts, experiences, and actions taken.

As for thoughts, I let fear come and go. Accepting fear is now a part of my journey. Up until that point, I ran from it—so I stopped running and gave fear a place to be in my life. I'm not stuck with fear anymore and it doesn't run me now. It's here to teach me something.

The action I take is...no action at all. I am just present to fear now. Fear wants me to react, to start surviving it, right here and now. But I can just be with the feelings and experiences of fearfulness. And when it comes, and I acknowledge it, it's gone in seconds. Having no resistance to fear is the key to having a powerful relationship with it.

I now experience powerful body sensations. There is a hollowed out and cleansed feeling from having a new and open space in my being—a space in which anything can emerge. Anything—and everything—is now possible.

Invitation to Reflect

———

Life is a journey and everything in it is part of the journey. It's not about whatever happens happens (as in "that's the way it goes"), it's about what happens, happens for a reason, reasons that we may never understand. There is a trusting in the journey, which is filled with stepping stones and endless opportunities for lessons to be learned. There is freedom and power for you by accepting life as a journey, and being responsible for the energy that is sourcing it. Will it be fear or love energy?

In this way of being in life, there will be the ability to freely choose, as opposed to things having to be a certain way. In life as a destination, there's no room for mistakes, and hence, no room for growth. It's black or white, success or failure. While both are important in learning life's lessons, often we learn more from failure. I know it will not be easy to make the shift from a life of destination to one of a journey.

My invitation for you is to take on this exercise. Write down all of the goals you want to achieve and the destinations in where you want to get. You may have already arrived at some while others are still out there waiting to be had. Wherever you may be, write them down and try to connect to the energy source that has you wanting to accomplish them in the first place. There is nothing more to do than just write them down and observe. Are they coming from a source of fear or love?

———

Invitation to Reflect
NOTES

_____

_____

_____

_____

_____

_____

_____

_____

_____

_____

_____

_____

_____

_____

Invitation to Reflect
NOTES

_____

_____

_____

_____

_____

_____

_____

_____

_____

_____

_____

_____

_____

_____

_____

_____

Invitation to Reflect
NOTES

CHAPTER 17

WHAT LOVE WILL DO

For months, I practiced forgiving myself for allowing so much of my life to be controlled by fear. I decided to monitor myself closely to see if I could identify the exact moments when I was being controlled by fear. If I could spot fear in the act, maybe I could have a shift. I made it into a daily practice, looking over my actions and continually asking myself—did I just react to fear? If I did, I was brutally honest with myself without engaging in self-blame. I remember when it finally happened—the instant when I sensed that fear is here, right now.

I was at work with my business partner, Alex, a fellow Israeli. We were sitting in my office, listening to our employee, Missy, tell us that she was leaving the company. As she divulged her reasons, I suddenly felt a tidal wave of emotions surge through me. It threatened to drown me, and I began gripping the arms of my chair. What was this? I was in the grip of fear. An employee was quitting and this triggered a tsunami of terror. My fear of abandonment was raging. It was happening right then, and for the first time, I caught it in action. It was a most appreciable moment indeed. Something about my being able to see it and name it allowed me to be with it and accept it. I did not make it wrong, I was just being with it as it was. I was able to put some distance between me and the fear. From my vantage point, I could examine my reactions. Why was I so terrified?

Even though I had not been particularly close to this employee, as she was not a dear friend, nor had she been employed long, I realized that I was terrified of being abandoned. And then I saw a larger pattern. I was as terrified of doing the abandoning as I was of being abandoned. That meant that as the owner, I had often kept poorly performing employees longer than I should have. I could not be with the fear of letting them go. As long as I perceived it to be a rejection to someone, or from another, I would be triggered and react. My heart rate would skyrocket and I became a hostage to fear. I saw it all so clearly—my hijacked nervous system, my palpitating heart, my sweaty hands. It was as if I were viewing myself from outside of me.

The very moment that I resolved to look my fear in the eye—rather than bury or disown it—it vanished. One moment it held me in a death grip, and the next, it evaporated. I searched my psyche for some sense of fright, but there was none to be found.

We see fear as something to overcome, dreading that it will paralyze us—which is exactly what transpires in trying to overcome it. And that is the conundrum.

In an instant, I came back to the room and became present to our soon-to-be-former employee. I got ever so present (as in a powerful listening) to her, her reasoning, the situation, and most importantly— validated it all. I saw horror in Alex's demeanor and his reaction to her leaving was one of desperation.

"Look what we did for you, how could you leave?" he bellowed.

We had flown her to California to attend a seminar that was an invest-ment in her career, so Alex had made a valid point.

"What do you need to stay?" he pleaded with her. "Can we give you more money?"

It occurred to me that Alex was fearful of losing his campaign to keep her and he looked to me to say something. He had an expectation that I would react as he had, and that's how I would have reacted before my awakening. My actual reaction, or lack of one, came as a surprise to us both. When I inquired if she had been happy here, she replied that she had not. So I said that she might find a job that better suited her elsewhere. Then I shook her hand, and wished her luck in her next endeavor. We hugged and off she went.

Alex was not happy with how I handled the situation. But I had let her go easily because she wasn't mine to keep. She was on her own jour-ney and I had a trust that everything would work out for us all.

While Alex continued to work, I went for a walk, amazed at how I felt being in the moment, connected to my new energy source. It occurred to me that I was listening from love instead of fear. There was a peace, and I felt enriched somehow about letting Missy be as she wanted to be, without anything in it for me. I had been invited into my soul so I could witness the energy source that had me choose love. It was unfamiliar territory.

Fear is a key component of the human survival machinery. It esca-
lates, billows, and mushrooms. It comes from a belief that whatever
is happening is a threat to one's survival. Fear had shaped my entire
life, controlling all of my choices and actions from the time I was a kid.
If I merely looked at it squarely, it lost its power and dissipated. If I
noticed what was happening as it was occurring, gained some distance
from it, and could then turn and face it—it would evaporate.

I began making peace with fear, but my life did not change drastical-
ly. I was just more aware of how and when I could be triggered and
I became less reactive. Fear still came, but when it arose, I caught it
in mid-stream. When I realized I was in fear, I paused and acknowl-
edged it. I did not run, instead chose to greet it. I kept opening myself
to the true energy of each situation, to see it for what it actually was.

I asked myself, was this really something to be afraid of? Or might
this be an opportunity for new growth and change?

Slowly but surely, I began to feel the change in my reactions, thus
feeling more connected to life. For so long, fear was in charge, calling
all the shots. It was vastly freeing to stop acting based on fear. And
there was something even more powerful that I could do. I could act
out of love. I could look at any situation and ask myself—what would
love do?

It was as if I had been sitting in the dark all my life and someone
had suddenly thrown the switch. Instantly, my being was filled with
illumination. Just thinking about the question—what would love do?
—I felt my heart swell with something spreading through my body. I
tuned in to myself, checking in on the old cascade of frightful emo-

tions. Instead, there was warmth, peace and joy. Just how long had it been since I had experienced any feeling remotely akin to joy?

I began practicing this in earnest—notice fear rising in the moment, pause, turn toward the fear, and ask myself—what would love do?

At last, I was finally finding a sense of peace in my life. It took so long to get there, or almost no time at all, depending upon your perspective. When I look at it now, it feels instantaneous, but looking back, I see that it took my entire life to get there. What mattered was the exquisite sense of liberation I had begun to feel as I shed the shackles of fear, which led to my awakening to the healing power of love.

This awakening was not a cure-all. I didn't suddenly transform my every thought, fear or emotion. When life showed up with obstacles, problems and confrontations, fear would be there automatically. But as I began to develop my sense of awareness to the fear, I could feel a sense of freedom—ever more and ever sooner—and I suffered less because of it. This sojourn continues to this day, and will until my last.

I talk about love, as opposed to fear-energy. So what is love energy? Love is a place of acceptance, of caring and action, peace and humanity, feelings and emotions, and a way of being—like being joyful, being light, being easy with people, considering others, showing kindness and respect, and having compassion.

Invitation to Reflect

————

"Between stimulus and response there is a space. In that space is our power to choose our response. In our response lies our growth and our freedom." Viktor Frankl, German neurologist, psychiatrist, holocaust survivor.

This quote from noted Holocaust survivor, Viktor Frankl, speaks to me so clearly. It is the space, the moment, to choose a response out of love. The actual choosing of a response is no easy task. Our survival mechanics has us react in an instant, and for good reasons—safety. But then we get to see how we reacted, and alter our future reactions if need be.

During the day, slow down every 3 to 4 hours and ask yourself; what was the basis of your reactions for the last few hours?

Did you come from fear or love? This takes some effort but the result is a great awareness. Then reflect on those reactions you just had. You will begin to see their energy source. Your ability to choose your energy source before reacting will increase. Eventually, you'll be able to notice in the moment which energy is sourcing you. In the moment, you will be able to choose from love. Be present to the fact that while you are immersed in fear, you cannot choose from love.

Invitation to Reflect
NOTES

_____

_____

_____

_____

_____

_____

_____

_____

_____

_____

_____

_____

_____

_____

_____

_____

Invitation to Reflect
NOTES

_____

_____

_____

_____

_____

_____

_____

_____

_____

_____

_____

_____

_____

_____

_____

_____

Invitation to Reflect
NOTES

Invitation to Reflect
NOTES

CHAPTER 18

LIFE AS A JOURNEY (REBORN)

In having this awakening, something in me began to shift. If I could be with the journey just as it was, I could *be* with whatever was, in that moment. This kind of thinking is found in many disciplines and practices such as Buddhism, yoga, meditation and transformational conversations. However, it is one thing to hear it or read it, and yet another to have it exist in *your* being, in your consciousness, in the background sourcing your actions.

Relating to my life as a journey gave me peace and strength. I was no longer at the mercy of my circumstances or at the affect of life. I could affect life itself, shaping it as it was unfolding, and accepting whatever was happening on my journey. It used to be a battle to understand the reasons for the physical and emotional pain in which I had languished, but then I no longer resisted it. Acceptance was part of the journey, with all its apparent triumphs and defeats.

There were so many goals and destinations that I wanted to reach. For one, I wanted to walk without a limp and wanted to make money. I wanted to find a wife. I wanted this, I wanted that, I wanted it all. But if I wanted to walk without a limp, that meant that my current walk was not good enough. The same with having money or a relationship—it meant that I was not satisfied with those areas of life as they were—or were not. I needed it all to be some other way.

Then something about that state of wanting no longer felt authentic. I had been living my life as if the most important thing was to arrive at a destination. Then I discovered that it's all about the journey. I had been needing something *out there*, something outside of myself to complete me. But as I began accepting my life as a journey, I set in motion an acknowledgment of myself as I already was. This included me walking with my limp. As I took on accepting myself, I included others like my parents, Sophia, Nicole—everyone—and I did so without judgment.

This journey of acceptance was a gradual process. Finally, one day I had the answer to Dalya's question…"If this is as good as it gets, would I be okay?" Yes. If this is as good as it gets, I will be okay.

From the beginning of this journey, to help me climb out of the deep morass in which I had found myself, I reached out to others. I had, without being conscious of it, commenced to assemble a team of helpers. It began with Patricia and then Carlos, Nora, Peter and Dalya, all who were more spiritual in being than I. They were my angels, my support, and I loved them dearly. They helped me through it. Their influence opened me.

Dalya had done more than just teach me to read. Our conversations had been so enlightening that I gave her the moniker "my Buddha coach." I don't even think she was a Buddhist, although the first book she gave me to read was by the Dalai Lama. Patricia used to say that I built Team Joel to save my life. She may have been right.

Being accepting of the reality of my physical condition, I continued to assemble members of Team Joel when I met Ron in 2014. Ron was an engaging and observant man in his mid-life who was a specialist in body movement. I told him that I wanted to address the quality of my walking, but if it did not improve, I would be okay. I shared this with him at a time when I could barely walk. He demonstrated exercises and taught me how to move my body. It was a challenge for him because my particular situation was not in his textbook, so he had to create a treatment tailored for me. We worked with a combination of muscles—stomach, leg and glutes—moving one leg at a time. My glutes and stomach muscles were so weak on my right side, I had to shift my weight to the left and then lift the entire right side of my body forward.

For most of us, walking is automatic—an innate action. We don't have to think about it. For me, I had to be intentional about how to move my body in order to walk efficiently. I had to contract my core and fire off my glutes in order to keep my foot from scraping along the floor. It was a full-time occupation just to be mobile.

Ron was extremely talented. He was all about building a strong connection between the brain and muscles. He guided me every step of the way and nothing about his approach was rigid. If I could not accomplish something, he would revisit his mode of operation and take me in another direction, using different muscles to reach the next level.

As we worked together, my right side grew stronger. I could see and feel the difference and I was thrilled. I didn't want to stop, yearning to push myself as far as what seemed possible. So I challenged myself to run in a work-related event... a 5K race. I was inspired by this challenge. With Ron's help, I began a rigorous training. I found that I could utilize this time for meditation as well, which left me in a very peaceful state, even though I was pushing through occasional pain.

On Thanksgiving Day, 2015, after a long and arduous training regime, I completed the race, which I found absolutely exhilarating. So I set a new goal of running a 10K by the new year. This seemed daunting but Ron knew how disciplined and driven I was, so we continued to train for this next level of my physical and personal development. And my newfound strength gave me the physical power to deal with all of the demands of life. Working with Ron was part of my journey to rebuild myself. He was an amazing person. Sometimes I marvel at the chain of events that brought him to me.

After my mom died and Sophia left, I experienced major sleeping issues. Being desperate for sleep, I opted for medication. When meds had little impact, I went to see Peter, hoping that acupuncture would make a difference. Peter referred me to David, who gave me several myofascial massage treatments. It was David who suggested that I work with Ron.

In sum, if the sleep medications had worked, I would never have gone to see Peter, and in turn, David nor Ron. Through the lens afforded me by this serendipitous chain of events, I began to see something very important—how naturally and easily life could unfold, with everything happening in the way it was supposed to. Before that, I could never have imagined such a thing. Looking back, I'm sure that life had been trying to happen in this manner but in living such a fearful life, I simply could not let it.

I do not think it had been an accident that I had to learn to walk all over again. After all, I was in the process of being reborn, of pecking my way out of the eggshell that I had built around myself. I was like a newborn—learning to breathe, feel, walk, and express myself. I was learning how to live again. This reinforced that life is a journey—and how everything truly is connected.

Invitation to Reflect

In a life of destination, things from your past may appear as mistakes, accidents, and, "this should not have happened, or it should not be this way," etc. But in life as a journey, these same occurrences present themselves as stepping stones to where you are now, and not as things you wish would have been different. In life as a journey, you can see the chain of events that has led you here, right now in this moment, reading this book. You can look back and connect the dots of your life and see the trail you have traveled to get here.

You can acknowledge that the fear energy you have been living with has led you to everything that has happened in your life and has brought you to this moment. With that awareness, now you can open yourself to a love energy, which will shift your outlook—and in turn, shift your actions, and in turn, shift how you can affect and impact your life.

Some of you may not want to be here right now. Your journey to this point has been hard. But know that this has been an integral part of the journey. These things happened for a reason. This is a moment for you to experience that. There is growth from this point forward. No need to blame others or yourself for the past. It's been your road traveled all along.

Now the doors to growth are open right in front of you. What will open up for you going forward? Be unbarred and curious as to where you may be headed. As you begin to accept your life, begin to accept people around you as well, as they are on their journeys too.

Invitation to Reflect
NOTES

Invitation to Reflect
NOTES

_____

_____

_____

_____

_____

_____

_____

_____

_____

_____

_____

_____

_____

_____

_____

_____

Invitation to Reflect
NOTES

Invitation to Reflect
NOTES

CHAPTER 19

TOWARD HEALING

After the exhilaration of running the 5K race, I ran a 10K the day after Christmas of 2015. I could not run fast but I never quit. I was blown away at my accomplishment. Running that race had taken a physical toll on my body, but the impact on me was a boosted stamina, improved physical capabilities, and a stronger mind. It confirmed that I was not handicapped. I saw that I could overcome anything, affirming that anything was possible.

During this long arduous race, I had time for reflection, and saw my tremendous level of daily stress. Raising two kids while exorcizing a volatile Nicole from my life was challenging to say the least. If one is enduring a high level of stress over a period of time, it exacts a huge toll on one's body. I could see that my stress was chronic and had begun in the first grade, and had never subsided.

I perceived that life was stacked against me, which left me stuck in survival. Because my body had been in life-long survival mode, my neurochemistry was completely out of whack. Stress had weakened my immune system, which increased my gluten sensitivity and created inflammation. This produced lesions on my spine, leading to the diagnosis of MS. Again, the thought had crossed my mind—*if I made myself sick, then I could heal myself as well.*

I thought that happiness was not an option for me. I never considered happiness at all. I thought it came from material objects and social standing. Then I had another realization. I never imagined that happiness came from within.

I had been living in a constant state of fear since I was a youngster. Being afraid was familiar—toxic—but familiar. Keeping this terrible energy in my body eventually made me ill. My body and soul were screaming but I did not have the capacity to hear.

Back when Dr. Shaw gave me his prognosis, I developed a game plan. I took supplements and focused on what to eat and drink. The *doing* aspect of healing came quickly because I was a doer. That opened the door to wellness, but it was just an opening. The spiritual aspect was the closer, something that had been missing all along. I saw the physical aspect of my illness, but the spiritual connection came only when I was completely broken and had asked: *How did I get here?* Only then did I begin to ponder why I became ill in the first place and what a spiritual connection could provide.

Recently, I was asked if the problems I faced were physical, emotional, or spiritual. I did not think I had any spiritual problems because in the past, I had no spiritual connection. In truth, I did not consider my emotional well-being either. I lived life in an unconscious state.

The pain in my back should have been a wake-up call. It was a communication that my body was angry at me for not dealing with my fears. The pain had escalated until it became unbearable and finally grabbed my attention. Because I was unconscious, I took no responsibility for anything that occurred in my life. I was not aware I had any choice in the matter. Everything I did was a reaction to something I was too afraid to deal with.

I believe that our bodies carry the potential for disease, which can develop when something in our experience causes it to emerge. For me, it was the suppression of my needs—emotional, spiritual, and physical—that allowed multiple sclerosis to take hold. I know that I had dietary issues as well but I am certain that if I had not suppressed my needs for so long, the disease would not have been able to take root and flourish in my body.

I would feel paralyzed when I was afraid. I am specifically using the word "paralyzed." It is no accident that I was diagnosed with MS, a disease of the central nervous system that can cause paralysis. My body had become accustomed to restricted movement long before my diagnosis. And yet, there I was, overcoming an obstacle that I never dreamed of—running a 10-kilometer race.

Invitation to Reflect

Reflect on your stressful situations and see what toll stress is exacting on your being (mind, body, spirit, emotions, behaviors, and so on). Be kind to yourself in this inquiry. No need to judge yourself. This is a space of curiosity and discovery.

In addition to the circumstances of life that can be a source of stress, we often create stress out of the thoughts rolling around in our heads, due to fear. Living in survival mode will keep fear and stress in place.

We often think things are real (as in my thoughts of "abandonment" and "not good enough"). But that may only be an interpretation of some underlying justification as to why something is. What is the underlying conversation that has us reacting this way about a situation? There will be a fear that drives our thoughts. And even if the situation resolves itself, the stress remains, continually impacting us.

As an exercise, write down what stresses you. Just stay with what you have written, and in due course, it will all unfold unto you. Again, no need to judge yourself.

Also, I invite you to meditate, which can aid you in this quest. In meditation, I use a mantra, which you will find in the last chapter of the book. In this chapter entitled "Affirmations," you will find a section "Treasure every moment, every breath." In this section, the use and purpose of the mantra is explained.

Invitation to Reflect
NOTES

_____

_____

_____

_____

_____

_____

_____

_____

_____

_____

_____

_____

_____

_____

_____

_____

Invitation to Reflect
NOTES

_____

_____

_____

_____

_____

_____

_____

_____

_____

_____

_____

_____

_____

_____

_____

_____

Invitation to Reflect
NOTES

Invitation to Reflect
NOTES

_____

_____

_____

_____

_____

_____

_____

_____

_____

_____

_____

_____

_____

_____

_____

_____

CHAPTER 20

HEALING CONVERSATIONS

In the summer of 2016, I sensed that something was awaiting me, that my life would soon shift in a major way, and I was content to let it unfold organically. Eventually, the moment came and it had a considerable impact on my life. That moment has led me to do the work I do today and is one of the occurrences that has inspired me to write this book. I cannot express in words the profound consequences of the following evening.

On this night, I began to notice the fear in others and realized that it wasn't just me who dwelled in emotional incarceration. This confirmed that fear is universal and it wasn't just me lacking something. I noticed it specifically when I had spent time in Israel visiting my daughter.

One weekend, Talia and I were invited to attend an event at an ashram in the desert, close to the Jordanian border. On the first night, there was a lovely ceremony filled with music and dancing, and love was ever-present. As I watched this affair unfold, I noticed one man in particular. He was obviously not Israeli, speaking only English with a heavy Italian accent. He was very muscular and quite handsome, with a macho appearance. He seemed to be strutting his stuff. I surmised that this was a self-absorbed guy who spent hours in the gym building his body and peering in the mirror. And yet, he was dancing and hugging people so lovingly. Something about this scenario seemed incongruous and I was intrigued.

The following evening, while Talia and I sat out in the star-filled and moonlit desert night, I saw that same man stroll by. Despite the late hour, I wanted to learn more about him. When Talia retired to her room, I introduced myself to him and we entered into a conversation. He was Adam, a massage therapist from New York.

I took the opportunity to share with him what I had observed during the ceremony the night before, and how touched I was by the love that he carried for people. He was visibly moved and we began speaking on a deeper level. As I was so intrigued, I asked him of his past and what kind of life he had led. Adam told me that he had left home when he was seventeen years old to make his way in the world.

"I lied about what I do for a living," he blurted out, as he grew more comfortable with me.

"So what do you do for a living?" was my question.

"I actually run an escort service," was his admission. "I have both male and female prostitutes.

I was struck by the fact that he was quite open and proud of this occupation. I had an immediate judgment, but I let it go so I could be present to the conversation.

"I'm a good boss and I treat them very well," he boasted. "First, I make them promise to leave the business in five years. Meanwhile, I invest part of their money in real estate so that if they leave, they have a place to live and money in the bank. Thanks to me, they will all be rich and happy."

He sounded almost parental. In my experience, pimps were characters on TV and in the movies, who were low-lifes and hardly loving to others. I had never met a real pimp so I wondered how he got into this profession. His natural athleticism and good looks led him into male striptease performance, and ultimately into prostitution. After he divulged his story, he began asking questions of me —who was I, what did I do, and what was going on in my life? I shared my journey, about the energy awareness work that was emerging in my life. When I began explaining the importance of fear energy and how it can shape all of our decisions, he challenged me.

"What does energy awareness mean?" he asked.

"There are only two energies that source our lives—fear and love," I replied. "Every moment of life, we operate on the basis of one or the other. Most of us react out of fear."

"I don't know what you're talking about," he defended himself, as I noticed his body stiffening. "There's no fear energy in my life. Look at me, I'm strong and have no fear of anything."

It was clear to me that my point had been made, as I found his body language and response to be fearful. I noticed that he defended him-self around the fear aspect but never offered up a defense that he was loving. Despite my observation of him being just that, he never took the opportunity to declare his lovingness.

"You have no fear of anything? Is that really so?" I inquired, in a man-ner that was non-confrontational, yet straightforward. "When I asked what you did for a living, why did you lie to me?" I had a sense that he didn't want to revisit his past.

"I was…" and then he stopped speaking.

"You were… what?" I pressed.

"I was afraid you would judge me," was his disclosure, and the expres-sion on his face was one of recognition.

"You've been succeeding in life," I said, "but you haven't been choosing freely, never having faced your fear, just being a reaction to it."

After he absorbed my statement for a few moments, I saw in his expression that there was an invitation to continue, so I posed the following:

"It doesn't matter that you lied to me, but why do you lie to yourself? You're paying the price for that and the time will come when the price will be too high. I know this because it happened to me. Fear had run my life since I was a kid, and as a consequence, I lived a great lie.

"My life of lying consisted of living with a shameful secret, so I used deception, manipulation and coercion to keep my secret, and survive my life. Eventually, the price I paid was a physical, emotional and spiritual handicap. Now I practice openness and vulnerability, no longer needing to keep my secret.

"Now Adam, I view you as living two lives. Here you are living in this ashram, engulfed in spirituality, a life sourced in love and caring, being parental to the people who work for you, the people you actually seem to care about. Yet look at how you make a living. Based on everything you have shared with me, I ask you to consider that your life is still sourced in fear, exemplified by the exploitation of these same young people that you care about.

"Fear requires you to have power, the power over others. Building your body is just one way of exerting your power. And here you are, prostituting these people so you can exercise your fearful power. You are still being sourced by that fearful kid, who eventually ran away from home, and is still running."

Then I shared my story with him, the story of my running from anything that might have me read, or becoming like my father—violent, dishonest, detached, and fearful.

"I sold my soul until everything fell apart," I confessed. "That's when I realized that I was very far from peace."

That seemed to have struck a chord with him. There appeared a weariness in him and he shook his head.

"I know," he sighed, "living at the ashram helps keep me sane because I know that what I'm doing for a living is wrong. I know it's wrong here," as he pointed to his head with a sense of defeat. "But I can't stop. Maybe one day I'll get busted and sit in jail, then maybe I'll wake up."

"I don't think that you see the entire circle of your life. Why are you an escort today?" I asked point-blank.

"Well, I had been a dancer and I saw that I could make more money as an escort," he said. "I was already using my body as a dancer to lure women so I might as well go for the big bucks. And it made me feel manly," he added, with a bit of guilt.

"How did you become a dancer?" I asked, peeling away the layers of his onion.

"I was a body-builder and I had gone to Vegas for a competition, and met a man who offered me the opportunity to dance for an all-male revue," he explained. "He said that I would be awesome and could get any woman I wanted."

"And how did you become a body-builder?" I asked again, as I continued to connect the links in his life's chain.

"Well, I love working out and how it makes me look," he said with a smirk, "and women love a ripped body."

"Do you remember the first time you went to the gym?" I questioned.

"Yes I do," he muttered, as his eyes began to water. "I was seventeen and ran away from home because I was afraid of my father. I promised myself that I would be so strong that no one would ever be able to hurt me again."

There was a long, almost deafening silence. His eyes closed and I let him soul search. It seemed like a lifetime of reflection for him and I could tell that a storm was churning in his marrow. Tears emerged.

"My father was abusive to my mother and me," he recounted. "It was a very unhealthy situation. I remember the abuse toward my mother starting when I was nine. In my mind, I knew it was only a matter of time before it was my turn. For the next eight years, I lived in terror."

He began to sob, with a body language that made him literally shrink in size. Adam's situation finally had gotten out of hand, where his dad was beating him constantly, until he beat him senseless. His mother screamed in horror for her son. This was the last time he would take this barbarous abuse. He was skinny and weak and feared for his life —running away from home, never to return.

He lived on the streets doing odd jobs and gravitated toward people with whom he felt safe, those who were bigger and stronger. This led him to ingratiate himself with the body-building crowd. No one would ever hurt him, nor would he ever fear anything again. Or so he thought.

"I see now where I've been living in fear my entire life, sort of like what you described," he mumbled, as the tears subsided.

"Think about your entire life as being a reaction to fear," I added. "You are still being sourced energetically by that terrified nine-year-old. When we have a fear event in life, we can only be with it for a half-second before we go into survival mode and start reacting to the fear. We never complete this cycle of fear. Automatically, we are looking for a way out. It might be by running away, or by hiding out, or by being aggressive, or by acting out in some other unsavory way—anything to ease the overwhelming feeling of fear.

"When we're willing to face that fear, our lives can change," I went on. "We just need to go back to that moment when that one kernel of fear was first planted when we were young, and feel what we felt in that very moment. It's getting reconnected with that one moment, and then staying with that moment, and that feeling for 30 seconds. Of course, that half-minute can feel like a lifetime. But if we can just be present to those feelings for those 30 seconds, the feelings will begin to transform. We can finally release that fear, and then amazing things can happen."

He looked at me dubiously.

"All it takes is 30 seconds... and a lot of courage," I finally added. We both laughed at the recognition of the need for courage.

We talked all night and I could sense that this was a bit overwhelming for him, so we hugged and parted company. I watched him walk away, backlit by the rising sun as the desert night gave way to a new day. His body was very healthy and he had an amazing heart, but there was a lot of darkness in him, and his soul needed healing. I was comforted in knowing that we made a connection, but more than that, I was left moved and empowered by this conversation.

I knew that it might take him a long time to make changes in his life, but I left knowing that a door had been opened. Given how long my own journey had taken, I did not expect overnight changes in how he would live his life, but I knew that I had an impact on him. It was my hope he would continue to walk through any open doors that lay ahead.

Through that intimate conversation with Adam, a new door had opened for me. I found a clarity in knowing that I am not the only fearful person. I had no prior relationship with him, and yet I could see his fear and its source. This was my first experience outside of my own life where I could see the fear connection of another, their reaction to that fear, and the control it had on their life. Experiencing this gave me confidence to take on the work that I do now—making a huge difference in the lives of others.

I found my life's work in this connection with Adam. I saw that I could profoundly impact others and their lives by sharing my awareness—through my experiences around fear energy. Until then, I had supported others mainly in their physical healing by sharing my own physical recovery inside of MS. Watching people choose a life of freedom from a source of love—rather than fear—is an overwhelmingly joyful experience.

Invitation to Reflect

I would like you to take on this amazing, yet sometimes harrowing exercise—of being with your fear for 30 seconds, This exercise was not designed to be easy but I promise you the reward of freedom once you connect to the moment. We are looking for that one moment when your life had been kidnapped by fear. From that moment on, you've been living in a reaction from that fear. Just seek out the experience of fear and relieve it for a half-minute or so. Surrender completely (as in giving up all resistance), and relive your childhood experience.

Take your time and go back to the early memories of your childhood. Can you see any events that shaped your life? In Adam's case, it was watching his mother get abused and then his own physical abuse. What was your event? How did you survive it? What survival mechanism did you create? And what did you tell yourself about the world, your relationships, and yourself?

Fear lurks in the subconscious, impacting your mind, which drives your actions, determining your results. Breathe in and breathe out, letting this experience complete you energetically. It may take multiple attempts to release the energy of this experience, Be patient with yourself, be loving to yourself, give up judgments, and accept the journey.

Invitation to Reflect
NOTES

Invitation to Reflect
NOTES

Invitation to Reflect
NOTES

CHAPTER 21

DOORS TO FREEDOM

Looking back at my life, I see what a miracle it is, and I am grateful for every day. I will not tell you that the journey was easy. There were long periods of stress and sleepless nights. Keeping everything together during that time—running a business and being a single parent—was a tremendous struggle. But then again, I was wired for struggle. My whole life had been built around overcoming adversity. Without an ever-present struggle, who was I? Struggle was my identity.

At the start, I did not realize how difficult this journey would be. I could not foresee where it would lead me, or how far or deep I would travel. Nor did I understand that it would require giving up all of the illusions of how my life should look. For two years, I was in a kind of chrysalis, in which I went through an almost alchemical transformation. During that process, I learned that ever since I was a kid, I saw myself as a survivor. That identity had hardened around me like an eggshell. But am I here only to survive? Absolutely not. I believe we are here to learn about life and to live freely. There is freedom available to those who are willing to go through their own awakening.

It is now my life's work to inspire and support those on this journey. I am available to bring awareness to others in finding the fear energy that is sourcing their actions. While I cannot break the eggshell for others, I can offer some thoughts based on my experiences. I think of these as life lessons, and doors that open to the path of freedom.

As I look back at my life, recalling the stories that I've shared with you, it seems like they never happened. I carried it all as weight, and now that I am free, I have no sense of it being part of my life. Of course, those events did happen and they shaped who I am today, but once I became complete (total acceptance) with those experiences, I stopped reacting with, *I'm not good enough* or *I'm stupid*, as my source. They no longer run me, as I am aware of the energy source that drove those ways of thinking.

One of the things that I had to let go of was the survival mechanism of control. When I refer to control, I am speaking to the notion that all of life had to be directed in a certain way. Every move or step was choreographed to achieve a safe outcome, and all of it in place to cover up my great secret—that *I am stupid* and I can't read. I created an entire life around this. It was a constant way of living that took a heavy toll on my body, spirit and mind. It was living life as a place to get to. I was living life as a destination.

In contrast, when I gave up the need to adhere to specific steps in life, I began living life with acceptance. I chose to accept myself as who I already was. I got complete on this...*I am stupid*...story. It became irrelevant as to whether I was stupid or smart or any other way. There was no need to control how things went but to accept how things would work out. I began to shift gears from *life as a destination* to *life as a journey.*

It has been both exhilarating and painful, this seven-year journey of personal discovery. But writing this book has been life altering. In it, I have experienced a profound love and commitment for people to free themselves from the shackles of fear. Having to face my fears in writing has been both frightening and freeing. And although I'm being sourced by love to write this, fear is lurking.

From my experiences, I now know what is available from this priceless journey of mine, and I encourage you to dive into yours. Perhaps something in my story will capture your heart and you will see what is available from the energy of love. Since I no longer live a life of destination, this project is unknown to me. I have no idea what the future holds, so there is a complete freedom here. I know nothing and I am detached from any outcome. Of course, I want you to get great value from my work, but I'm not attached to it. And it excites me that the next generation will have this resource to fuel the energy of love. I've never felt this way before, I've never been in this place or space before, this is all a new frontier for me.

Invitation to Reflect

————

When I work with clients, around the second or third session, I ask a novel question which usually sparks a weird response. I ask, "Do you love yourself?" Clients often do not respond because they never have pondered such a question. The notion can induce feelings of being self-centered if they do, and it may come at the expense of others who then won't get their fair share of the person's love. And often, clients do not feel they deserve this self-love.

Wherever you are in your life journey—and hopefully the work that you've done in reading this book will give you an opening—you will be able to understand the question. And no matter how you answer the question, please keep asking yourself on a daily basis. Do I love myself?

What does it look like in loving yourself? Consider everything that you do or don't do in life. Look at every thought, choice, action and reaction. What do you eat, drink and put in your body? What do you put in your mind? What do you tell yourself about yourself?

When you love yourself, you create a conduit to loving others and receiving love in return. This cycle of love leaves one with a harmonious life. Experience this love cycle everyday. My invitation to you as you complete this book is to be aware of your source while asking the question... am I loving myself?

Invitation to Reflect
NOTES

_____

_____

_____

_____

_____

_____

_____

_____

_____

_____

_____

_____

_____

_____

_____

Invitation to Reflect
NOTES

_____

_____

_____

_____

_____

_____

_____

_____

_____

_____

_____

_____

_____

Invitation to Reflect
NOTES

_____

_____

_____

_____

_____

_____

_____

_____

_____

_____

_____

_____

_____

_____

_____

_____

_____

_____

Invitation to Reflect
NOTES

CHAPTER 22

DAILY AFFIRMATIONS

This chapter contains a bevy of affirmations for you to reflect upon and return to for later reference. You will find these as tools you can use throughout your life. In my work, I use these tools every day with clients and with myself as well. I utilize these affirmations as a guide to living a full and free life.

While some readers may find these points inspiring immediately, others may absorb these affirmations over time. With practice, as with anything, there will be a shift from what was—a life of surviving—to a new life of freedom and power.

As you progress through these pages, the Invitations to Reflect that ends each chapter, may seem inaccessible or confusing. This is natural since many of you will be taking on—for the first time—a journey such as this, that differs quite a bit from your life of destination. So I have brought them here, along with some other powerful distinctions, in one final chapter called, Daily Affirmations.

It's easy to get stuck on some of them—as to what they mean, or how they should be used. Please let go of this need to understand them. Just be with them and absorb them. They will come to you, and this chapter will assist in that. Use this chapter for a reference.

This first affirmation is probably the most powerful of them all for a foundation of a free life.

EMBRACE YOUR LIFE AS A JOURNEY (AND LET GO OF CONTROL)

My healing journey started years ago and continues to this day. In this, I have discovered two opposing ways of living life.

Life as a destination is one way to live. In this strategy, success and failure, and good and bad, are somewhat defined. Life is goal-oriented...and there is a cost to living life in this manner. The design here is to be successful, well-liked, and in control. This often provides a sense of security.

In general, people are driven to living life toward a particular end point. We find ourselves self-molding, to become someone that we desire to be. Yet we remain unfulfilled because life *should* look a certain way. We *should* have had these things already, or *should* have them in the future. *Should* is the constraining word here.

The other way of living life is... as a journey. This is a diametrically different way of living and *being* in life. I used to resist life, where anything and everything had to have controlled outcomes. Now I accept things as they are, and as my relationship to *self* has strengthened, I am more accepting of my past. This new found ease is the key to accepting anything ahead of me, provided I am willing to give up control. This is not just settling for things but an acceptance of things. I have shifted my relationship to life's circumstances. Now I view situations and occurrences, not as obstacles, but as opportunities to learn and grow and evolve in my thinking and *being*.

I became intentional in giving up control by simply being accepting of the journey. I gave up my attachments to those controlled outcomes which were rooted in fear. Before, I was fixated on how my home should or should not look, whether my finances were plentiful, or if my relationship was in danger. Everything had to look a certain way that left me feeling safe. Fear had a grip on me without my awareness.

When you let go of having to steer all outcomes in life, fear will lose its grip and power over you, and your reactions. That brings you the freedom to choose to live from love. In the space of love resides the power to accept life as it comes, which ushers in joy, fulfillment and peace. The circle of acceptance to love and love to acceptance is complete.

When I share with others that I am now relating to my life as a journey, some say that I have surrendered (as in defeat). For me, it is not about surrender. I have a great power in how my journey unfolds, and I can actually shape its course. Before, my focus was on some goal or destination. And now, I just let life unfold before me, shaped by me, sourced by love.

In sourcing my life from love, I am open to the opportunities that life presents to me.

Relating to life as a journey means that I accept my life as it is now and I am grateful for it. I know that life has its own rhythms and pulses, and constantly changes. I fully accept myself now, including all of life's challenges, however they are and may evolve to be.

GIVE UP CERTAIN WAYS OF BEING

Living this journey only became possible when I altered my relationship to *all* of my past—*all of it*. In the process, I found a new freedom. But there were things I had to give up to get to this place. One was the giving up of *being right*.

I had plenty of agreement in the world about how wrong Sophia had been, in all that she had done in our marriage, especially her ultimatum when I went to be with my dying mother. But in giving up *being right*, I saw that making her wrong no longer served me. It kept me angry and there is no freedom in that. When I let go of that "rightness", (or righteousness, if you will) I let go of the anger. In *being right*, I am closed, and see no point of view other than my own.

For most of us, there is too much vulnerability in being wrong and it is too much of a threat. Being wrong in life is akin to losing in life, and we will do anything—anything—to not lose. *Being right* has us feel safe, but that is just an illusion. *Being right* provides us with a feeling of control in a battle that needs to be won. To humans, *being right* and avoiding being wrong is more important than anything in life.

Another way of being for me to give up, was *being a victim*. I was a victim because I had MS. I felt less than complete, which left people feeling sorry for me. My family, friends and co-workers had low expectations of me, therefore, I could not disappoint. I became special, as people would feel for me. And since I came from a place of, *I will overcome this* (because that's who I am)—people will see me as a hero.

In *being a victim*, I was able to be so right about how I had somehow been wronged. Before I had my awakening, just getting to zero was an accomplishment. If the game of life were played from one to ten, then I dwelled in the red, so getting to zero was a victory. Since I thought I was stupid, how could I ever get to ten?

When I gave up the victimization, I became free. I no longer had a limited view of myself and what I could accomplish. As a stupid person, every little thing I did was a great achievement. The usual, the common, the ordinary—were all mountains climbed for stupid Joel. I lived a very small life. There were no real breakthroughs, no great levels to rise to. It was all baby steps. When I gave up *being stupid*, I stopped judging and comparing myself to others. No longer feeling less than, I became free to grow and take on any of life's challenges.

Another way of being was to give up *being manipulative,* which came from the need to control. I had to use manipulation to accomplish my goals—calculating and maneuvering to mold my desired outcome. It was an exhausting experience, utilizing so much mental energy to steer things in the direction I wanted. When I released my desire to control life through manipulation, I found an enormous sense of freedom and power that I had always been seeking. There was then room for peace, trust, and faith in my life.

As I gave up these *ways of being* in my past, there was this profound sense of emancipation. All of these past incidents and experiences prepared me for the rest of my journey. Without them, I would not have these insights to share with you on living a complete life.

When I work with people in a coaching capacity, I suggest that they consider shifting their relationship to life. Instead of focusing on desires and goals in their future, and perceived happiness at arriving at some imagined destination, I urge them to center on the journey itself and consider giving up control of anything and everything.

We are often trapped in living a life of destination in search of happiness. Happiness is not a destination but a by-product of the peace one gains through acceptance of life as a journey, with all of the obstacles contained therein. Through acceptance, there is a place of peace for happiness to emerge. For example, I would often think to myself, *I need to walk without my limp, I need to make money, I need to find a wife.* I was focusing on the lack of something. I was telling myself repeatedly that I am not complete as I am right now, and I need something more to complete me. Those thoughts dissolved once I began living in a space of acceptance.

There is now a sense of strength, peace and fulfillment (happiness) in my relating to life. I have an acceptance of faith, and I experience a sense of power with no attachment to the end result. I have the ability to accept others wherever they may be in their lives because I understand that others are being sourced by fear themselves. The value here is that nothing is as meaningful as it once was. I do not attach meaning to things that are said or done that I might have previously taken personally. I can now savor, revel in, and celebrate the moments of life along the way.

HEAL FROM THE INSIDE OUT

For years, I just did what needed to be done—exercise more, eat this and avoid that, eliminate certain behaviors, and so on. It was a lot of doing, as in actions taken. I related to myself and to my body as separate entities. My body was just a vehicle. There was no recognition of my emotional and spiritual side. These entities were not of concern and need not be nurtured, nor did they seem to have any particular impact on my physical health. While I had significant physical healing through these prior actions, some limitations remained due to my lack of intentionality on my *way of being*—a missing link in my healing.

My old way of *being* came from a place of surviving and overcoming, which was familiar territory. When I tapped into my spiritual side, it was scary, intimidating and uncomfortable. Yet I was able to release stress and fear, which aided my body in healing itself from within, in a most powerful way. When I addressed my emotional *self* and embarked on the more spiritual aspect of *me*, I reached another level of awareness.

I have found a distinct awareness inside of meditation and other synergistic disciplines. When I guide my clients through meditation, I am aware that they do not relate to themselves in a nurturing way. They have a certain detachment from their mind, body, and spirit. They tend to eat and drink and consume in unhealthy and non-nurturing ways. And not just consumption through the mouth, but also through the mind.

We read, watch, and listen to negative information and influences that come from many forms of media, which offers zero nurturing for the mind. The mind is a strange place, and whatever thoughts come from there will determine our actions. Since we operate mostly from fear, our subconscious mind does as well. When I meditate, I try to bring awareness to my subconscious, which can then influence my mind, and therefore, impact my actions and results.

I key in on my breath, which is my key to meditation. I'm okay with the thoughts that come and go in my mind, and just get back to my breath as soon as I become aware that thoughts are coming and going. I use a four-word mantra when meditating—a repetition of love, compassion, kindness, and health. When I speak and breathe these words, they impact my subconscious. My mind, body and spirit become one.

When people use this four-word mantra, they begin to relate to themselves in those ways: love, compassion, kindness, and health. Once the meditation is complete and they open their eyes, tears often flow as they have a new experience of themselves. Having this new experience of oneself is the conduit to transforming from a life of fear and destination to a life of love and journey.

Once individuals have a new experience of themselves, they become present to the fact that they have not related to their bodies in nurturing ways. They no longer relate to their bodies, their minds, and their souls, with blame, unworthiness, anger and disappointment—all emotions sourced by fear.

I do not expect people to free themselves after their first meditation, but its continual practice will open the doors to eventual peace, serenity, ease, and love. They will have a choice as to which energy source will source them—one of fear or one of love.

TREASURE EVERY MOMENT, EVERY BREATH

When I breathe these four words: love, compassion, kindness, and health, I close my eyes, inhaling through my nose, and I imagine that with every breath I take, I'm filling my body with love, kindness, compassion and health.

From my arms and hands to my legs and feet, from my fingers to my toes—my face, my ears, my internal organs, my spine—all of my body dwells in this fulfillment of the energy of love. When I breathe out, I'm surrounding myself with the same love energy.

When I breathe in kindness, I fill my body with the kindness that stems from loving myself.

It fills my mind and soul. When I breathe out this kindness, it envelops me with an energy sourced by love.

When I breathe in compassion, it fills my body and mind with acceptance as to where I am in my journey of life, and to where I may be going. I am releasing my self-judgments and my judgments of others. Breathing out this compassion allows it to encompass me.

When I breathe health into my body, I am thankful for the healthy body that I have.

I breathe with a specific intention to areas of my body that need extra support.

When I breathe out, I surround my body with health.

I repeat these exercises one word at a time. I will stop intentionally throughout my day and simply breathe these words to keep me balanced and present. I breathe them in and I breathe them out. It is a way of cherishing my body, spirit, and mind.

While meditating, it occurred to me that we humans take our breath for granted. We can live without food for up to five weeks, without water for a week, but without breath for only a few minutes. Yet, we are consumed by what we eat and drink, while taking our breath automatically. Of all the breaths we take in life, over 600 million, perhaps we are profoundly impacted only by the first and last.

When my children were born, they started life with that first gasp of breath. It was a thrilling moment. I've also witnessed the passing of both of my parents, and each time, they took that last gasp before finding their peace. These were precious moments. I've come to realize that each breath, just one of millions we will take in our lifetime, is quite monumental. From the first to the last, and all in between, each breath is priceless and irreplaceable.

Often, we are so caught up in life (and it's great meaning) that we don't realize *the miracle that we are* in taking each breath. I did not experience this in my past while living in fear, and now I just slow down and appreciate the gift of taking a breath. It reminds me to be grateful for the gift of life.

BE WILLING TO BE VULNERABLE IN ORDER TO ACCESS FREEDOM

The willingness to be vulnerable is one of the most important openings to freedom.

Many of us spend a great deal of effort learning how to protect and defend ourselves. That's exactly what I did but the cost was enormous. I was so protected inside of my eggshell that I could not let others in. I was defensive, detached and isolated.

I thought *being vulnerable* was *being* weak. The paradox is that it is the strong and courageous who are vulnerable. Only when I was truly vulnerable and authentic with myself, and others, could I undertake the difficult task of acknowledging the impact that fear had on all aspects of my life. We can be truly vulnerable and at peace with ourselves when we have a great level of self-acceptance.

There is a vast difference between vulnerability and acting vulnerably—the latter having us be manipulating and looking good. I often thought that I was being vulnerable when actually I was just saying and doing things to manipulate life. An example is when I lived guarded and in perpetual conflict with Sophia, just wanting to feel safe and be at peace with her and my kids. I was willing to do and say anything to keep that relationship, so I contemplated, calculated, and manipulated every move in order to appear vulnerable. I admitted my flaws and weaknesses (yet did nothing about them) as a way of surviving.

Living in the space that I just spoke of has no freedom, joy or peace. But when we reveal what is in our hearts and authentically share ourselves, we create the possibility of acceptance and are able to transform any relationship. We can also leave relationships, if wanted, through the same vulnerabilities.

Then there is the opposite of *being vulnerable*, and that is *being* guarded, protected and covert. In my case, I was guarding and hiding my big secret. I often wondered what people thought and said about me, because in my mind, I felt stupid. But in being vulnerable, there is no issue with wondering what people think—it's a non-factor. The conversation of whether I am stupid or a genius no longer sources me or my self-reflection. Living without secrets is the access to freedom.

When we reveal our vulnerabilities, there is no longer the need to hide or pretend to be someone we are not. Letting down our guard allows us to take off our masks and create an opportunity for healing—leading to inner peace and its rippling effect. It allows a space that gives others the courage to take off their own masks.

ACCEPT YOUR FEARS

Some part of me knew that the fearful, defensive, manipulative, constrained, and unhealthy life that I had been living for 45 years was not the life I really wanted. It was no life at all, so this forced me to grow and change. It obliged me to realize that out of fear, I had built a wall around myself—a metaphorical eggshell.

I thought I needed it to protect me from the world, yet I was blind to how it was isolating me, stifling me, and preventing me from growing.

Life did everything it could to wake me up, to help me recognize how much my eggshell was costing me. Life sent me disease in order to heal myself. It sent me heartache and loss to enlighten me in accepting my vulnerabilities. Life sent me the most inspiring supporters, teaching me to care about others, and reminding me how much I wanted and needed a deep connection with humanity.

Finally, life challenged me to break out of my shell on my own, giving me strength and understanding that I was stronger than my fear. It is not that my fear has disappeared. None of us can ever be completely free of fear. It is just one state of mind, and when it comes, I accept it—no longer running away.

Most of us do not realize how much of our lives revolve around avoiding fear. We assume that we are freely choosing our actions. Actually, we are simply reacting to the fear lurking in the background—invisible, yet shaping everything we do.

One example is when Alex and I faced Missy, our employee who chose to leave the company. My fear of abandonment kicked into high gear and I was in its grasp. I realized where I was listening and reacting from—fear of course—and was able to be with it in the moment. I made peace with it while Alex was in full survival mode, looking to me to smooth things over. This was a familiar role, as I came from quarrelsome parents where I often acted as the peacemaker. When my parents fought, fear told me that the family unit was in danger of breaking apart.

Fear can be very subtle. It creeps into our *being* and impacts our listening of others. We judge them from our place of survival, always attaching a right or wrong, or a credit or blame. In the process, we skip being responsible for ourselves and our own perspective. Once we become aware, we can let go of our judgments.

I coach people in reconnecting to their life-altering moment when fear first occurred. This moment may be quite significant as in a past abuse, or as insignificant as in a childhood rejection. Whether sizable or slight, this moment is still shaping their life. What keeps sourcing their ongoing experiences is the fear they felt in that moment.

As a coach, I guide them through the reconnection to the emotions of the experience, so they can re-experience the fear they felt when it first occurred. That fear is still strong because it was that pivotal moment in childhood that indoctrinated them into being fearful. When they relive the moment and see how it is still impacting them, they can transform it.

Through meditation and that reconnection, they can complete the experience of fear that never got completed in its original occurrence.

This is the moment in which they can make peace with fear and the experience that has shaped them, that sources their reactions.

When you sense fear, turn and face it directly for a period of time. Recall the feelings you felt in that original fearful moment and stay with them for a half-minute or so. There is nothing else to do but to stay with the feeling for 30-40 seconds and see what opens up. This is no easy chore. Your survival will immediately kick in and look for the easy way out. But when you are willing to feel fear, it alters—weakening, and eventually collapsing and vanishing—and you can be left with a feeling of freedom and inner peace.

GIVE UP YOUR SECRETS

We all carry secrets about ourselves that shape our reality. I had lived my life as though I were really stupid because of my secret dyslexia. That was my reality. The dyslexia was real, the stupidity was not. I believed that I was not good enough and I guarded that secret with my life. When I came from a place of *I'm not enough*, I was limited in experiencing life as a journey. I was guarded and constrained, disconnected from myself and others, making it impossible to live my life freely.

Some secrets are created by our own fears. In my case, I hid Nicole's addiction from my family, for fear of what they would think of me. I had no one to support me through all of my crises with her. I was on my own, and that left me unable to fulfill on a free life.

Then there are the secrets we carry resulting from external events, like sexual abuse for instance. This can impact and shape the victim as they move through life, with some feelings like: *I did something wrong, I'm bad, I'm ashamed, I was irresponsible, and I am guilty*—and there are many other feelings that may arise. A secret like this carries very heavy weight, requiring a person to perfect their own survival methods. All of this stems from fear energy.

The breakthrough here is to open up the secret, first to ourselves and then to others. The amount of fear energy we carry to protect the secret is very high. The amount of physical and emotional energy we expend in hiding the secret is very great. In the carrying of the secret, we create a reality for ourselves that is based solely on hiding the secret.

BE AWARE OF YOUR JUDGMENTS

One day while meditating, it occurred to me that there were certain statements that I took at face value. One of them was, "don't judge a book by its cover." This is conventional wisdom, but during meditation I found this statement to be judgmental itself. The statement seemed to imply that after we've gotten past the cover, and now that we have read the book, it is fine to judge.

I believe we react out of fear, and we judge the actions of others who equally react to fear. If we have compassion and understanding of others, we will not have to be right about who they are or how they think or what they do, which keeps us disconnected from them. It's just their expression of where they are on the journey of their life, for reasons that are beyond our ability to know. And like fear, judgments will always be there automatically. It's the awareness of the judgments that will make the difference.

We view others through our filters, understandings and experiences, but when we take the time to view others through compassion and kindness, something else becomes available. Through awareness, judgments will lessen, and as they do, our connection to people rises. My view is to always be aware of your judging others—and of yourself.

LOVE YOURSELF

Love your neighbor as yourself. While I was meditating one evening in a Buddhist temple north of Pittsburgh, for some odd reason, this adage popped into my mind—*love your neighbor as yourself.* What does that proverb even mean? I had never given this much consideration before my awakening. Most of us have a difficult time loving ourselves, so if we love others as we love ourselves, there would be little love to go around. We can hardly give what we do not possess. Only when I love myself can I give my love to others.

As I pondered this, it came to me that the statement should read: *first love yourself, then love your neighbor as you love yourself.* So I began asking my neighbors and others this question: *do you love yourself?* Very few had said yes. Some say that they can't love themselves because that would be selfish. They have kids, a husband, a wife, those who need that love. I believe that it's impossible to truly love others if we don't love ourselves. So practice loving yourself. For most of us, this is very challenging because we often think that others are more important than ourselves.

In loving myself, I take care of my physical, emotional and spiritual well-being. I surrounded myself with those who support me in growing. Every day I do something just for me. With so many hours outside of sleep, there can always be time for oneself. It can be a five-minute meditation or a ten minute walk, or eating a good snack— something where only we ourselves derive benefit. It's a small step to take but worthwhile, and it points us to the right path.

If you can find that acceptance and completeness of yourself, you will find more love to give to others than you could have ever imagined.

EVERYTHING YOU DO, DO FROM LOVE

My work is all about how we relate to fear and love, which are opposite forms of energy.

Earlier in this text I said that love and fear cannot coexist in the same space. There is no capacity for love if we are filled with fear, and conversely, there is no space for fear if we are infused with love. To live from a foundation of love, we must make peace with fear.

Some time ago, I was coaching a woman who was immersed in a custody battle with her ex-husband, who had moved to another state. She was terrified of losing her kids due to the fact that the previous hearings did not go in her favor. I suggested that when facing the court, she come from a space of love, and not from fear. I invited her to focus on how much she loved her children and not on her fear of losing them. Suddenly, her demeanor changed. It was clear she had shifted out of a fear-based region of her mind and into the love in her heart. A sense of peace emanated from her face. Later, she reached out to me, thanking me for the difference this had made for her way of being in court. She had been able to show the judge her true self and how much she loved her children. She was quite surprised to find the outcome in her favor.

BREAK THROUGH THE EGGSHELL

I believe that the path to freedom requires us to break out of our egg-shells continually throughout our lives. By "eggshell" I mean all the restrictions and constraints that we put on ourselves due to our protection from fear. We can choose the safety of the eggshell of course, and just stay protected, but then there is a price to pay—a limitation in life's experiences.

For some of us, breaking the eggshell is a life experience all its own, making us stronger in the process. For others, life's circumstances force us to break through or suffocate. For me, those circumstances were Sophia and my mother. These were life experiences forcing me to grow. I grew wings and now have the freedom to fly. I am no longer engulfed by the familiarity of protection.

Of course, new eggshells form constantly and automatically out of the fear that is running in the background. Having the awareness that these shells are forming is key. This cycle of forming and breaking through the shell is exhilarating. This exercise is not easy and all of us can use support, but there is a part that only we can do on our own.

When we come to that moment, fear will be running the show, but life has ways of sending us exactly what we need when we need it to learn a life lesson. To see it, we only have to have the awareness.

CHOOSE FROM LOVE

Even with the acute awareness that I have developed over a great period of time, at this moment, I find that I am in great fear. It encompasses me, wreaking havoc on my entire body. Here I am, writing a book about fear, and now I am wholly immersed in it. I see that in writing this book, fear has unleashed its unyielding power on me—but not over me.

Here is what I am present to: *What will people think of my book? What will they think of me? Will they be moved and inspired by my work? Will they judge my beliefs, ideas and ideals? And what about the people that I speak of in the book? Will they be angry? Will they still think I am stupid? Will I be abandoned in some way?*

I have just meditated and have become confronted by these thoughts. What I am left with is that I no longer have my secrets. I've kept them for a lifetime, and now that I have shared them with the world, I will never be able to take them back. And that, I am at peace with.

Fear will never leave me—this I know—so there is no point in trying to resist it. In the past, I would have been paralyzed from fright, but now, I am just frightened—and nothing else. Now I have choices in how I want to handle fear. I am amazed at how swiftly fear has arrived—in just a matter of a split-second.

As I said earlier in this book, if I can make myself sick from fear, then I can heal myself with love. So if fear can arrive in a split second, then it can disappear almost as rapidly. By acknowledging it, and being with it, before you know it, before you even realize it, it's gone—that is until it shows up again spontaneously in the next moment, or with the next life challenge.

What I have learned from my journey and in my work with others is that I have the choice of fear or love. So I choose love. Whenever I am aware, I will choose love. When I am frightened and aware of my fear, I choose love. Fear is ever present, and still I choose love—as long as I am aware. Awareness is the key to making the choice between fear and love.

I choose to complete this book. I choose to open myself, and to share my secrets. And when I do, I am instantly free.

And what of those earlier questions? *What will people think of my book, what will they think of me, will they be moved and inspired by my work, will they judge my beliefs, ideas and ideals?*

Then let me ask more questions. *What if only one person on the planet, just one, gets value and heals themselves, or creates a new-found relationship with self that did not exist before, or restores their relationship with another (or is able to end it in a complete way), or overcomes their struggle with self-esteem, or gets to the other side of a learning disability, or starts living a fulfilled live with freedom from fear?*

What if? Then all of my work and all of my shame and all of my secrets revealed will have been worth it. Through acceptance, I am okay with being vulnerable in the face of fear.

If you are that one, that has been touched or moved to action by this work, then please write to me or contact me through social media or at www.theeggshelleffect.com. I want to hear from you.

I thank you for your courage and humanity. I love you even though we may have never met. Now I choose to operate from love and love only. Fear will be ever-present, but I choose love.

To all of you with love and respect,

Joel

CPSIA information can be obtained
at www.ICGtesting.com
Printed in the USA
BVHW070705071020
590455BV00003B/6